# Why Your Writing Sucks

## Business writing that works in the digital age

## MARCIA ROSS

ISBN: 1516839897
ISBN-13: 978-1516839896

# **Contents**

# Introduction

The way you were taught to write didn't prepare you for the world of work today.

You began with writing fiction and stories (perfect preparation for the one-in-ten-million who becomes a fiction writer). You progressed to academic essays (ditto, for the one-in-ten-thousand who becomes an academic in the social sciences).

But that wasn't such a big issue, because most professionals didn't write much back then. Office/white-collar workers did most of their communication with each other and with clients through a thing called talking. In person and on the phone. Even in those comparatively rare instances when a letter or written report was required, a good deal of the work was performed by an under-employed secretary.

In today's professional work world:

- Writing is how things get done
- Writing replaces many of the conversations and phone calls of 10 years ago
- Your reader is inundated, all day long, by things to read.

In my 20 years as a professional writer I've come to believe that most college-educated people are unconscious apostles of tired old writing gods. I wrote this book to help you leave that old-school thinking and move to a more practical paradigm.

WYWS isn't a textbook. It's not about writing rules; it doesn't involve memory work; it avoids lectures on grammar. It's a philosophy of writing, an approach designed for the digital workplace.

As a believer in Pareto's Law, which you may know as the 80/20 rule, I've focused on the most common errors I see every day. 80% of poor writing stems from the same 20% of problems. Address this tiny 20% and you will have solved 80% of your writing issues.

You'll learn how to:

- Write more clearly

- Be more productive, by transferring suffering-time to editing

- Increase your business value, by becoming a better communicator.

Let's go.

# 1. Why does your writing suck?

## What defines bad writing?

What's the standout quality that makes writing bad?

**Bad writing is *written for the writer*.** Not the reader. **Good** writing delivers what concerns the reader. As concisely as possible.

Following, a comparison of *reader-focused* versus *writer-focused* writing. We'll be returning to these later, but take a boo now. Note: bad writing can be grammatically perfect!

| Writer-focused | Reader-focused |
|---|---|
| BAD | GOOD |
| Includes *any relevant* fact | Includes only required facts |
| Builds to main idea | Starts with main idea |
| Wordy | Cut to the bone |
| Hard to follow | Easy to follow and understand |
| Stiff, formal, often uses big words and passive voice | Simple, breezy, direct. Starts many sentences with "You" |
| Proud | Humble |

Below, writer-focused versus reader-focused versions of the same message.

## ~~~~~ Examples ~~~~~

No: In the aftermath of the recession and in response to continuing uncertain economic conditions, many organizations have felt the need to cut expenses. At times talent management programs have been the platform to target human capital resources as the initial opportunity to realize economies and expense management. Boomers have had numerous experiences with these downsizing initiatives; it has made many reluctant or fearful to discuss future plans of their intentions. Most employees don't want to talk about retirement and managers are reluctant to raise the subject or ask the question about when an employee might be considering retirement.

**Yes**: Boomers have had many bruising encounters with downsizing. They've become wary of discussing plans or intentions with managers. In turn, managers are reluctant to raise the subject with these employees. And even more reluctant to come out and ask *when* an employee might be considering retirement.

**No**: Please fill in and return the attached form so that we can keep our records up to date.

**Yes**: To make sure you receive your dividends promptly, please take a moment to fill in the attached online form.

**No**: We will not be able to restore functionality of the new phones until each handset has been activated centrally. This process will be completed by Tech Central at extension #329.

**Yes**: Your new phone must be activated before you can use it. Please dial #329 to reach Tech Central; the activation process takes less than a minute.

~~~~~ ~~~~~ ~~~~~

# What kind of writer are you?

Having a better handle on the type of writer you are now will help you to figure out how to improve your business writing. None of us is exactly ONE kind of writer, but having an awareness of your tendency can be quite revealing.

*Fiction* serves to entertain.

*Academic writing* exists to further learning.

*Writing at work* AKA business writing, is boots-on-the-ground, practical, **persuasive**. It moves the process forward; you're persuading your reader to take the next step.

Take a look at the following table and then reflect for a bit. (I'll be here when you get back.)

Why does your writing suck?

| Type | Purpose | At worst | At best |
|------|---------|----------|---------|
| Academic | Further knowledge; impress other academics; get funding | Difficult, wordy, turgid | Clean, assured, informed, insightful. |
| Fiction | Entertain / stimulate / provoke. | Shallow and awkward. | Enjoyable and/or interesting. |
| Non-fiction | Inform / inspire | Heavy. Dry. Fact-packed. | Informative. Well-paced. Insightful. |
| Journalism | Inform; sway; argue a point. | Dull or shallow. | Interesting. Well-structured. Informative. |
| Business | Inform. **Persuade**. Move your client or colleague to the next step. | Pretentious. Airless yet windy. Cautious. Crammed with jargon-de-jour. | Clear. Structured. Purposeful. |

# Writing is how things get done

**Writing is how things get done**, in today's work world. If you can't get your reader's attention, or if people have to wrestle with your words, or if your colleagues avoid what you write, you've got a serious problem. Both with your current job, and your career prospects.

In today's business world, you're fighting for your reader's attention against tough contenders, every time you write. There's too much for people to read – the amount has increased five-fold since the 1980s (You receive **five times** as much information as you did in 1986, according to Dr. Martin Hilbert, University of Southern California.)

To put it another way:

*You're a chore or a bore?*

*You lose your reader fer shore!*

## 2. The 4 reasons your writing got this way

I believe that many people are aiming for a writing style that doesn't suit the work world of today. But they don't really realize what drives their choice of writing style. Once you have a clearer idea of why and how you were encouraged to write in a way that doesn't work, once you recognize the forces that may have been driving you, it's easier to shuck them. It's easier to adopt a new approach.

Q: What did the Dalai Lama say to the hot dog vendor?

A: Make me one with everything.

The Dalai Lama then asks the hot dog vendor the price of the hot dog.

The vendor says "Three dollars." The Dalai Lama hands her a twenty. She pockets the twenty, hands over the hot dog, and turns to the next customer. Perplexed, the Dalai Lama asks "Where's my change?" Without looking up, the vendor replies, "Change must come from within."

Four reasons, I've found, are at the heart of why people find it hard to write well at work. Let's take a look.

## Reason One: Miss Ledd misled you

Meet Miss Ledd!

Miss Ledd is all the elementary school teachers who taught you how to write, every one of them, plus some of the ones in middle and high too. Miss Ledd did her best with a thankless assignment. For most, it was like being hauled through a hedge backward. Many of the misleading myths about writing come directly from Miss Ledd.

### Miss Ledd got you early

Remember your 1st-grade photos? Mouth full of baby teeth / regrettable haircut / innocent gaze? Miss Ledd got you early and wielded enormous influence over your fledgling brain. But her focus was not crisp clear communication, nor persuasive writing. Over the years, it varied between teaching you how to be a fiction writer, writing stories, and how to be an academic writer, writing essays. Neither of which prepares you for the working world.

### Miss Ledd made you believe that …

Miss Ledd left you with the indelible impression that people want to read what you write. And that they read every word. Even though you know you don't like to read what other people write, this early impression is hard to shake. You carefully compose with the innate belief that people will read with the same effort that you put into composing.

But you and your colleagues and your clients all work in a distracting e-world now. Bore or confuse, and your reader will fail to absorb, or outright leave. Zap! You're off the island.

### Miss Ledd's sentences

Miss Ledd taught you to add descriptors, aka adjectives and adverbs. The goal was longer sentences, as long as possible. Remember?

- "Tara, what kind of dog was it? Tell me about the dog."

- "Mark, was it small or big? What color was it?"

### Miss Ledd's paragraphs

When my son was in eighth grade I helped him with a book report. It came back with a poor grade and a note from his teacher (yet another Miss Ledd) asserting that for good writing all paragraphs must be a minimum of eight sentences long. The note suggested that my son get himself a good editor.

That man has no idea how close he came to a

painful bout with reconstructive dental surgery.

## *The result of Miss Ledd's teaching*

The Miss Ledds reserved their highest praise for a series of large blocky rectangles of text, proceeding evenly down the page. Students who could achieve this beamed at their work with pride. No wonder, it's not easy to do!

The problem is that it's not easy to read. Repetitive dense blocks of text are uninviting, even forbidding. They're a prison readers are forced into and fear they cannot escape. Does anyone approach the reading of a legal document with delight?

## *The Miss Ledd legacy in high school*

High school teachers continue Miss Ledd's approach. Essays have a minimum word count! Exams incite wordiness – the marking scheme rewards the student who writes as much as possible, because such a student is more likely to hit on the available points in the marking scheme. There are no points for being concise, no demerits for wordiness, no requirement of a well-worded argument. Why not write as much as possible?

*The grammar-god gets glued in*

There's another result of teaching writing only as a process (do this this and this) rather than a task with a goal (get your point across). It's the entrenched belief that good grammar is 80% of writing. Raise the topic of good writing and most people's first thought – try this out! – is about getting the grammar right. It's about Not Making Mistakes.

Recently I listened to a CBC interview featuring Steven Pinker, who'd written a book on writing. No surprise, the radio host opened the interview with a prelude centered on grammar, writing errors, and getting it right. When she thought about writing well, that's what she thought about … all those terrible things that cramp your paws and freeze your brain and prevent you from getting any words down.

I'm not espousing poor grammar. I am saying that communication is key to getting things done in the modern workplace, and focusing on grammar is counter-productive. Quit paying obeisance to the grammar god, and begin worshipping the god of getting your point across.

*The final nail in the coffin…*

… is that we come away with a **need to impress** when we write.

Listen for it and you'll hear it constantly – that grisly bond that most educated people forge between writing 'properly' and being intelligent/educated. Decades on, we still hear the guidance of Miss Ledd. The warmth of her approving smile. The safety of her reassuring comments. At work, many people put more time into trying to sound intelligent than into making sure their reader gets their message. These people may not admit it, may not even know it. But it's sadly true.

*Solution?*

Bury Miss Ledd. Disengage yourself from her teachings and your fear of poor grammar. Focus on writing for your reader.

~~~~~ **Example** ~~~~~

### Original (from the 'About' page of a design firm)

The increasingly competitive corporate climate means that organizations need both strategy to reach their audiences and a unique and comprehensive corporate image in order to differentiate their organization. Effective design is a marriage of talent and strategy, and we deliver on both. We specialize in branding programs including corporate identities, business communications, packaging and websites. At Alliance Artwork a belief in simplicity, sincerity and integrity prevails.

**Improved**

A strong corporate image is critical to differentiation. At Alliance Artwork, we combine strategy, insight and talent to create powerful branding programs: corporate identities, business communications, packaging and websites. Throughout, a belief in simplicity, sincerity and integrity prevails.

| What Miss Ledd said… | How readers feel… |
|---|---|
| Write sequentially, starting at the beginning of your argument and proceeding to its conclusion. By the end of your message readers will have understood your point. | Does this have anything to do with me? I'll scan and skip. |
| Big words and long sentences are impressive. Adjectives are fantastic. | This is bloated. What's your point? |

| | |
|---|---|
| Nothing, but nothing, makes you look more intelligent than a series of boxy paragraphs of similar dimensions. | Do I have to read this? It looks so forbidding… \<sigh\> |
| Headers and sub-headers are ONLY for lab reports and science projects. Elsewhere, they are undignified and inappropriate! | Headers and sub-headers! Sweet!. |

## Meet my friend Nasrin

You've probably worked with people like the woman I'm about to describe, whom I'll call Nasrin. Her first language isn't English and she speaks with an accent. Sometimes her grammar or syntax are a touch dodgy, a little idiosyncratic, inflected by the rules of her mother tongue.

But!

You always understand what Nasrin says. Because she's clear clear clear. She's a born communicator. She knows how to get her point across.

Nasrin is the spoken proof of what I'm saying about written communication. It's not about the grammar. At work, you can do an excellent writing job without big words or perfect grammar. Good writing at work is about connecting with your reader, humbling yourself to provide the info they want, the way they want it.

So stop OCDing over grammar. Please. You're wasting company time.

~~~~~ ~~~~~ ~~~~~

# Reason Two: Wrong-headed management

A dark belief in dull text pervades the business world. The belief has endured for centuries, I'm convinced it's pre-Dickensian. It's only recently that the long arm of the Internet has had any success in toppling the bloated practices of business writing.

I've heard many reasons given for why the business world believes that business English should be stuffy and unappealing. My favorite is that English originally developed as a hybrid of two languages, Anglo-Saxon and Norman. Anglo-Saxon is more concrete and descriptive, while Norman is more abstract and refined. In Anglo-

Saxon it's smell, buy and brotherly; in Norman it's odor, purchase and fraternal.

The business world plumps unerringly for Norman words. They're removed from the grit and sweat of humanity! They sound so important! They're so long! We love them big words!

But really, the reason hardly matters. We live in a world where many businesspeople think that writing should be dull, stiff and ponderous. Nonetheless, the online world is changing that. Bulky writing fails online. Measurably. Miserably. And that reality is percolating though a world that is learning that communication counts in business. Big time.

## Reason Three: It's the editing, stupid

In 1992, campaign strategist James Carville was asked to work on Bill Clinton's presidential campaign. Carville came up with three phrases, one of which – *It's the economy, stupid* – gained considerable popularity. My variation – *It's the editing, stupid* – is a reminder that editing is the easiest way to improve your writing. Later, we'll get into this. For now, think of writing as a two-part process – composition and editing. Almost everyone who writes at work devotes too much time to the former, too little to the latter.

## Reason Four: Other-thinking is tough

Good writing is based on the reader's needs, not the writer's. It's humble. If you'd like to read more about this, check out David Meerman Scott's *The New Rules of Marketing & PR*, now in its fourth edition. Scott talks a lot about buyer personas. The idea of a buyer persona is that you write with a specific person in your mind's eye, rather than an abstract. In his foreword to *Buyer Personas* by Adele Revella (who taught him a great deal about the concept), he says: "Market using the voice of your buyer, not of your founder, CEO, product manager, or public relations (PR) agency staffer. This builds a bond of trust with your buyers."

You may be thinking: "I'm not a marketer!" But the concept is the same. In order to engage your reader, speak in a tone and language that is easy for them to absorb. A tone that's based on their needs and wants, not yours.

I admit, it's crazy-difficult to write for your reader rather than yourself. We come to writing with our own frame of mind, our own agenda, our own pressures. How do we get into the reader's head, think the way they think?

Of all the skills we'll talk about in this book, this one's the toughest. Stick with me, I've got some tips.

## Summary – why your writing sucks

Now you know the Four Reasons! You were led astray as a child; bosses and old myths aggravate this problem; you over-compose and under-edit; you're an incurable egocentric. How are we going to address all this?

Read on.

# 3. Composition: 7 actions to up your game

Let's start with composition. But note that writing is an iterative process involving composition *and* editing. You compose, you edit, you compose, you edit. We're starting with composition only because you can't edit until you compose.

In just a minute, I want to talk to you about 7 actions to up your game, to make composition easier and better. But before we do that, let's talk about how you *visualize* your reader. Bear with me, this will be quick. Then we'll get to the 7 actions.

## Visualize a *distracted* reader

Subconsciously, you tend to visualize your reader as undistracted, attentive. Even interested. Like Miss Ledd, or your Mom. Because that was your earliest, burned-in experience.

But writing for your intent reader is akin to campaigning for your party only in the towns where you could run a puffer fish and win. You're wasting your time; those folks are going to vote for you anyway. Or in the case of writing, those people will get your message anyway.

When I tell a client that their draft is hard to follow, or makes confounding leaps, they often say: *Yes, but the reader will work it out from context. Later on, I show them that* – and here they pause to stab a place in the hard-copy with a confident finger – *that we are....*

No no no! No they won't! They're just not that into you!

Communication is a courtship. Not a command performance. Your reader always has one foot halfway out the door, with umpteen tempting distractions to pull them further.

90% of writing at work is persuasive – you want to move your reader to the next step.

*You're a chore or a bore?*

*You'll lose your reader fer shore!*

## Action 1: Use short words

**You learned the short words early.** You heard them first. Spoke them first. Started reading them around the time you were losing your baby teeth.

Short words are **deeply** embedded in our brains. Your reader absorbs them instantly.

Longer words are later acquaintances.

Longer words *never* attain the same power and pungency as your old pals, the short words (unless you're Conrad Black.)

Absolutely, do use longer words, particularly for precision. They can also deliver color, style, and impact. Make sure you give them LOTS of air though. The more you pack big words together, one after another, the more comprehension and engagement drop.

## ~~~~~ Examples ~~~~~
### Too many big words

*Too many big words* We enable our clients to optimize their business through a combination of process investment strategies, technology leverage, and business process outsourcing and provisioning.

*Improved* We help our clients to increase profits by running their businesses more efficiently. Our strengths lie in process improvement, the ability to leverage technology, and knowing how and which tasks to outsource.

*Too many big words* All schools are committed to the delivery of a digital education to every student in the metropolis with a student-to-device ratio of 1:1.

*Improved* We are committed to digital

education. Our goal is to reach a student-to-device ratio of 1:1.

*Too many big words* We provide an integrated end-to-end supply chain offering from the initial concept phase – providing design and engineering expertise, new product introduction, supply chain design and commodity management.

*Improved* We provide an end-to-end supply chain offering. This begins with design and engineering support, moves from there to new product introduction, and then to supply chain design and commodity management.

~~~~~ ~~~~~ ~~~~~

Of course you understand every individual word in the "too many big words" versions above, right? You know what those words mean. But you won't easily get what the writer is talking about, even less likely that you will retain any of it. You may not even read it.

**Retention** is what it's all about, at work. Residue in your reader's mind. No retention – no residue – no forward motion.

~~~~~ **Examples** ~~~~~

I have a dream today.

—*Martin Luther King*

And yet ... it moves. (Eppur si muove.)

— *Galileo*

Use the small, old words that all people understand – words like 'right' and 'wrong' and 'justice.'

— *Janet Reno, American Attorney General*

~~~~~ ~~~~~ ~~~~~

# Action 2: Use short sentences

**Shortening sentence length** is the fastest route to better writing at work. Yet Miss Ledd's teachings die even harder than Bruce Willis; most business writers avoid or under-use short sentences.

Here are three reasons why shortening your sentences will help your writing:

   1. Shorter sentences are easier to write.

2. Shorter sentences are easier to revise and swap as you edit; your editing job is easier.

3. Easier editing makes for better writing.

For your reader, shorter sentences are:

1. Easier to read, easier to follow.

2. Less likely to strain your reader's *cognitive load*. Less daunting, more inviting.

3. Long sentences are filling jails with people who – uh oh! Maybe you're not a fan of puns…

## ~~~~~ Example ~~~~~

My friend Bob has a senior role in the public sector, with a staff of 30. I asked him recently: *What are the writing problems you see most?*

*Verbosity*, Bob replied instantly. *They take forever to get to the point. They go on and on and on and on. With run-on sentences like crazy! And too many commas. I tell them, don't worry about where to put the comma. Just write shorter sentences.*

~~~~~ ~~~~~ ~~~~~

*Cognitive load? Squeeze me? What's that?*

The theory of *cognitive load*, simply stated? Your brain's RAM is finite. Once you overtax it, the same things happen as when you overtax the memory of your computer. Things slow down and don't operate as well.

Long sentences increase cognitive load. They make your readers keep a number of bits and pieces of text in their heads as they read. It's tiresome when overdone. Particularly for today's impatient reader.

William Faulkner, American winner of the 1949 Nobel Prize in Literature, was known for his long involved sentences. And Faulkner did not lack fans. But fellow author Ernest Hemingway was not one of them:

*Poor Faulkner. Does he really think big emotions come from big words? He thinks I don't know the ten-dollar words. I know them all right. But there are older and simpler and better words, and those are the ones I use.*

Internationally-known marketing strategist and author Perry Marshall agrees:

*When your copy reads at a 5th grade level, it's primal. Gut level impact. It sails right into your reader's brain and sticks. Your reader* *spends his brain cells digesting your **ideas**, not your **sentences**.*

Finally, consider JK Rowling… Experts have discovered why even dyslexic children love the Harry Potter books. The studies suggest it is easier for dyslexic children to read her stories because she *does not stretch cognitive load*. She writes sentences that are easy to follow.

Try 'em! You'll like 'em!

### It's not so easy to write a sentence!

All this being said, it's not so easy to write a sentence! Whole books have been written on the topic. Do keep in mind though, that the most common reason, the 80% cause of ugly hard-to-read sentences, is trying to put too much into the sentence.

Here are 4 tips:

1. Stick to one main idea, with at most one sub-point. This can be tricky with complex concepts. You may fall off the simple-sentence wagon…

2. …But clamber back on! Beat down that clunky sentence – chop chop! Cut your sentences into pieces. Leave them as is, or rejoin them in new ways that work better.

3. Be ever-ready to throw in very short sentences. They add pace and dynamism. Readers love 'em!

4. Punctuation is bad news and good news for you as a writer. Commas and periods tend to stop your reader, that's the bad. The good is that punctuation makes your meaning clear. Use enough punctuation to make your meaning clear, but no more. Yes, I agree this is a tough assignment. But it gets easier when you keep in mind that clarity and ease of reading are your goals, not punctuation rules.

## Sentence length – number of words

*Plain Language* experts recommend that clear writing should have an average sentence length of 15 to 20 words. I'd argue that's a bit long. I stick to an average length of 10-14 words. There's no good reason *not* to use shorter sentences, and many reasons to do so.

Plain Language, by the way, is a movement to make business and government writing (particularly the latter) clear, concise and readable.

## Variety is the spice of life, when you're writing

Averages are funny. You can have a group of

people in a room whose average age is 42, yet no one is actually 42 years old.

You do **not** want to have most of your sentences coming in at 14 words. You want to vary their length. A mixture of short, medium and long sentences helps to hold reader attention. Let me say that again: **vary your sentence length** to hold your reader's attention.

Average number of words in the above two paragraphs? 12

Actual number of words in each sentence? All over the place – 23, 3, 15, 6, 13, 14!

*Fragments are just fine!*

You may have noticed already that many of the sentences in this book are not actually sentences – at least, not according to the way you were taught to write. Many are what mighty Microsoft Word would label as 'fragments.' So would Miss Ledd. "*So would Miss Ledd*" is a case in point. Not to mention some of the sentences preceding this paragraph, the ones that started with *Average, Actual,* and *All.* But…

**…Clarity, cogency, and reader engagement** trump grade-school grammar in the day-to-day work of communicating with your colleagues and clients. At work, your goal is to get your reader to understand and act on what you write.

Let's say that again: at work, your goal is to get your reader to act on what you write. There are no prizes for adherence to rigid grammar rules. **All** prizes go to those who earn reader engagement and move the work forward.

You'll find that once you relax the rules about sentence fragments [Yes, you can start a sentence with *and*. And I do it all the time] it becomes considerably easier to write engagingly. Try checking out the writing on your favorite web blogs or forums over the next few days. You may be surprised at how many 'sentence fragments' you find in the writing of highly respected, well-followed writers.

## Action 3: Use short paragraphs

I remember the day we first studied paragraphs in grade school. That year's Miss Ledd claimed that any given paragraph has a defined beginning, middle and end. That there was a clear, objective, undisputed place to break for any given new paragraph.

I think not.

Writing a paragraph is unlike, say, skinning a weasel. With a weasel, once you've skinned it, you know you're done. There on the one side, you've amassed a pile of blood, bone and guts. On the other, an empty weasel skin.

Whereas knowing when you've finished a paragraph is more like finishing a painting. It's a subjective decision. It can change. And it should.

You heard it here first! *You* choose where you start and end your paragraphs. There's no absolute right and wrong. The only rule I advocate for when to start a new paragraph is: **often**.

Your primary goal is clarity, but the second, hard on the first one's heels, is holding the attention of your reader. I'm *not* saying that paragraph beginnings and endings are random – you can only move your paragraph breaks once your document has achieved some level of clarity and flow. I *am* saying that your primary goal is to make your writing clear and easy to follow.

Also, just as with sentences, feel free to swap your paragraphs around. I do it with every single thing I write or edit. Including this book. Also, *vary* the length of your paragraphs. Some short. Some medium. Some long. Mix it up. Be like a baseball pitcher – keep 'em guessing – that way they'll pay more attention.

*Simplicity is a sign of truth and a criterion of beauty. Complexity can be a way of hiding the truth*

*— Helen Rubenstein*

While I'm editing, I often throw in new paragraph breaks to see how they look. If I don't like the result, I take them out. And then I try a different place. It's the work of a moment. It's easy to do and it will help you improve the appeal of your writing.

~~~~~ **Example** ~~~~~

See below. I took a huge ugly para I found on the web and broke it into smaller paras to make it more readable. It was the work of a moment to do so. Better? Yes?

### Huge ugly paragraph

Alfred Day (1810–49) first published this controversial work in 1845 to substantial negative criticism. He was encouraged in his enterprise by the composer George Alexander Macfarren (1813–87) who remained a staunch supporter of Day's theories. The work begins with an introduction to Day's new approach to the figured bass and then moves on to set out his concept of diatonic (or strict) harmony and chromatic (or free) harmony. Each is discussed in depth, with sections devoted to common chords and their inversions, discords, pedals and modulation together with a large number of musical examples. This second edition of 1885 by Macfarren includes an additional preface discussing the genesis of the work and supporting its basic premise, together with an extensive appendix presenting his additions and differences of view, developed during the intervening period. Despite its complexity, Day's thinking had considerable influence on later writers on harmony.

## 3 paras – see the difference?

Alfred Day (1810–49) first published this controversial work in 1845 to substantial negative criticism. He was encouraged in his enterprise by the composer George Alexander Macfarren (1813–87) who remained a staunch supporter of Day's theories.

The work begins with an introduction to Day's new approach to the figured bass and then moves on to set out his concept of diatonic (or strict) harmony and chromatic (or free) harmony. Each is discussed in depth, with sections devoted to common chords and their inversions, discords, pedals and modulation together with a large number of musical examples.

This second edition of 1885 by Macfarren includes an additional preface discussing the genesis of the work and supporting its basic premise, together with an extensive appendix presenting his additions and differences of view, developed during the intervening period. Despite its complexity, Day's thinking had considerable influence on later writers on harmony.

~~~~~ ~~~~~ ~~~~~

*So double down on two keys to improve your writing*

You can improve your writing by using two keys more often. From what you've just read, you may be able to guess what they are ...

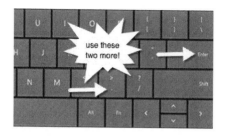

*Use your period key more often.* Shorten and simplify your sentences.

*Use your return key more often.* Shorten and simplify your paragraphs.

Nothing will improve the clarity and appeal of your writing more quickly than hitting those two keys more often.

## Action 4: Dive headfirst into headers

Headers are a double-boon, they aid both you and your reader. With headers, you can see at a glance if your writing flows logically and clearly. You might be thinking: *But I rarely use headers!* Ah, but that was the old you. Now, you do! Any time you're writing more than a few paragraphs, use headers. In reports, in minutes, in blog posts, in just about any internal or external written document.

What kind of headers? Meaningful ones! Your headers, read sequentially, should give an outline of your argument (see examples below).

For your reader, headers deliver a bursting piñata of benefits. They break up the text. They enforce more whitespace. They enable scanning (more on this later) and review. They guide your readers, helping them catch the flow of your argument.

## ~~~~~ Examples ~~~~~

**Weak header:** Issue

**Better:** Issue: Weak understanding of branding compliance

**Weak header:** Observations

**Better:** XD100 is outperforming the competition

~~~~~ ~~~~~ ~~~~~

# Action 5: Understand the power of the little joiners

http://www.theatlantic.com/magazine/archive/2012/10/the-writing-revolution/309090/

Let me introduce you to an article in *Atlantic* magazine that I came across recently. It's about the efforts of a gutsy, tenacious principal, Deirdre De-Angelis, who was determined to improve the woeful grades of her Staten Island high school students. After a number of failed experiments, she decided to focus heavily on writing, on how teachers supported writing inside each classroom, in virtually every subject.

She had an uphill battle on her hands; even her teaching staff were not on her side.

*"Although New Dorp teachers had observed students failing for years, they never connected that failure to specific flaws in their own teaching. [...] They were doing their job, they told her hotly. New Dorp students were simply not smart enough to write at the high-school level."*

Deirdre persevered. Starting in fall 2009, she decided that, if nothing else, New Dorp students would learn to write well.

Writing skills became a critical part of every high

school class (even chemistry!) except math. I'll tell you what happened, in just a bit, but first I want to focus on a discovery Deirdre's team made when they tried to figure out *why* motivated kids of normal intelligence couldn't compose even the simplest and shortest of essays.

After a few unsuccessful hypotheses, a history teacher and a consultant worked out that what the poor writers (most of them) lacked was flow, and that the lack of flow stemmed from ... coordinating conjunctions. Words that helped to link and expand on simple ideas—words like *for, and, nor, but, or, yet,* and *so.*

So the staff set up special lessons that taught the kids to use words like *although, despite, for, and, nor, but, or, yet,* and *so* in sentences.

Eureka! Not only did writing skills shoot up, grades improved across the board. The number of kids in programs leading to college-level classes rose from **148** students in 2006 to **412** students in 2011 (a 178% rise in 5 years!).

Moral of the story? There are two.

**Moral 1** Conjunctions are signposts that improve flow. They make it easier for your reader to follow your thinking. Adding a conjunction can make the difference between confusion and comprehension. And a bonus – using a conjunction can makes it clear to you, the writer, when your thinking isn't clear.

So don't skimp on the if, ands and buts! Use them to guide your writer through your thinking. If you'd like a summary of all the conjunctions out there, take a look at the resources section of wyws.ca.

## ~~~~~ Example ~~~~~

Below, the paragraph you read a page or two ago. You'll see that *but* and *even* give your reader's brain a heads-up on what's coming next. That heads-up makes the writing easier to follow, easier to understand.

*The article describes the efforts of a gutsy, tenacious high school principal, Deirdre De-Angelis. Deirdre was determined to improve the woeful grades of her Staten Island students. **But** she had an uphill battle on her hands. **Even** her teaching staff were not on her side.*

Weak: Annie loathed every minute of law school. She delights in her career as a civil rights lawyer.

Better: **Although** Annie loathed every minute of law school, she delights in her career as a civil rights lawyer.

Weak: We can draw lessons from the past. We cannot live in it.

Better: We can draw lessons from the past, **but** we cannot live in it. [Lyndon B. Johnson]

~~~~~ ~~~~~ ~~~~~

**Moral 2**: Sound, logical thinking is the foundation of good business writing. When your writing supports the use of joining words (*If* this, *then* that, *and* then we…) you're more likely to be expressing yourself clearly.

# Action 6: Seduce. Spoon-feed. Make it sticky…

**The ugly truth of business writing is the reluctance of your reader.** Your reader has too much to do in the day, with too much to read a considerable part of that. Following, a few proven methods to seduce and spoon-feed your reader into sticking with you:

**Conjunctions** As just discussed, conjunctions and connecting words take some of the hard work out of reading. When your reader has to work to follow you, you're halfway to losing her.

**Context** People need a framework that they can stick facts into. Without a framework, they have a random group of facts that they don't know where to store. Provide context **at the beginning**.

**Brevity** *Every reader* has an internal warning bell that instantly detects bloat. Once their bell goes bleep-bleep? You-the-writer are halfway off the island. Keep in mind, holding your reader's attention is *much* more important than being absolutely comprehensive. In fact, it's much more important than anything. If they don't read, it doesn't matter what you wrote. So decide on the *minimum* message you need to get across *now*, for *this* communication. Viciously, vigorously delete everything else.

Whenever you use two adjectives ("broad and thorough" or "forthright, honest"), one is often plenty. Delete the other. Be precise enough *for your purpose today*. Or as my mother used to say:

"Marcia, you don't have to tell *all* you know." Because every word you write is one more reason for your reader to stop reading.

My friend Zoey, whom you'll run into again later, says *But it hurts not to tell it all!* I know, I know. I hear you. Suck it up.

~~~~~ **Examples** ~~~~~

[From a book blurb] With new strategies for dealing with e-mail inefficiencies and practical tips on getting ~~and staying~~ organized, this book will free up hours of time each week ~~for what's really important~~.

True, *getting* organized and *staying* organized are not identical tasks. But "and staying" is not adding much. Your scanning reader will understand the message without it. Ditto with "for what's really important."

---

Recently I convinced a client to take the word *aspiring* out of the sub-title of her book: *Nuggets of wisdom for new and aspiring entrepreneurs.* "Aspiring" doesn't add, because any aspiring entrepreneur looking for a book will check out

46

one that is addressed to *new* entrepreneurs. Plus, *Nuggets of wisdom for new entrepreneurs* is considerably more euphonic, it rolls trippingly off the tongue. And yes, that does matter.

~~~~~ ~~~~~ ~~~~~

# Action 7: Tell a story

Many business messages are just congealed lumps of facts. While some parts may be useful, little is compelling. And there's no arc.

*Telling a story* is all the rage in the business world. For good reason. But what really is *telling a story*? And why is it a good idea?

Stories provide pace, direction and dynamism. You get a trajectory that starts and ends. You get a bit of color. You draw your reader in. Stories work because:

1.  Study after study after study shows that *we are feeling beings who think*, not thinking beings who feel (yes, even bright educated professionals start with their emotions, trust me on this). Reach your reader through the emotions, then justify your argument with facts.

2. We hear stories from infancy. They're in our skin.

3. What's an anecdote but a story? We use stories to communicate, all day long.

4. Most business writing divides the writer and the reader: *I the writer* tell or dictate, *you the reader* read and/or obey. But stories join us.

*After nourishment, shelter and companionship, stories are the thing we need most in the world.*

— *Philip Pullman*

*Why exactly do stories work?*

A blog called BufferSocial decided to get gritty about why stories work. They started by composing the same blog post in two different ways: one in a just-the-facts style, the other by using a story (http://blog.bufferapp.com/power-of-story).

Even card-carrying story-advocates were shocked at the results: the post with the story had nearly 300% more people scroll all the way to the bottom. Average time on page was *more than five times higher*! Given that a 10% improvement would have been enough to give pause for thought, 300% is enough to bowl one right over.

Next, they decided to find out why. Here's what they learned from a research study that monitored brain activity.

Patrick-the-participant is reading a story about Anouk. Lo and behold:

- When *Anouk* picks up an object, the neurons responsible for hand movements in *Patrick's* brains fire.

- When *Anouk* looks around her, *Patrick's* vision-neurons fire.

When we hear a story, our brain responds as if *we're in the story*! How's that for engagement?

No one is sure if Hemingway actually wrote one of the shortest and most famous stories in the world, below, but you have to admit it packs a punch...

"For sale:

Baby shoes. Never worn."

E. Hemingway

*A touch of humor never hurts*

Humor and stories go together like pancakes and syrup.

One day a mathematics teacher at an elite private school was trying to convince the school board that algebra was being taught at too early an age. He knew it would be a struggle to convince them. So he started with the (true!) story below, from his own teaching experience. It certainly got his audience listening, which is half the battle.

~~~~~ **Example** ~~~~~

"It was the second day of the algebra module," said the math teacher. "The first hadn't gone too badly but I still wasn't at all confident that the class was catching on.

"I started by working out a simple algebra problem on the blackboard. When I finished, I looked around, and announced brightly: 'So you see, X equals 4!' "

A sea of faces looked back at me blankly. No one said a thing.

Then a girl at the back of the class shot up her hand. I said, "Yes Jessica?"

"Just hold on a freaking minute!" she said. "Yesterday, you said X equals 7!"

~~~~ ~~~~ ~~~~

# A few more composing tricks

*Add a dash of colorful words*
"Watching Phil Mickelson play golf is like watching a drunk chasing a balloon near the edge of a cliff," says David Feherty, a popular sports commentator.

Lucky Feherty! If he were doing business writing instead of sports commentating, his colleagues might look askance at him. Like a family of shrews, say, in a discussion of Junior's Poor Behavior, Ill-befitting A Shrew.

But you don't need to be as dull as the Senior Shrews would have you be. You can add a dash of color with word choice. Use words that the average writer avoids but the average reader knows.

Keep your own running record of words with flavor, such as:

Daft. Deft. Juicy. Sweet. Tinker. Swoop. Barren. Trounce. Gleam. Sting. Gritty. Warrior. Glutton.

Use them. You'll note that the top business bloggers are not dull writers. Ditto for those who write the kind of non-fiction books that actually get read.

## *Bicycles, cheese and snakes*

Studies show that your readers remember concrete, tangible words better than abstract ones. Readers recall words like *bicycle*, *cheese* and *snake* better than words like *distribution* or *incentive*.

Whenever you can, make it real and concrete. You'll get better traction. And you'll develop a rep as an unboring writer, which means that your colleagues will approach writing from you with a positive attitude and pay attention to what you write.

Similarly, specific trumps generic. Reader-centered writing uses the specific, not the generic.

## ~~~~~ Examples ~~~~~

**No**: The workshop offers a full breakfast.

**Yes**: We start with strong fresh-ground coffee, seasonal fruit, protein, and tasty pastries.

**No**: We're having challenges in keeping package-contents within specs on #10 cereal line.

**Yes**: We're giving an extra 6% to our customers that we aren't charging for ... maybe we should register as a charity!

**No**: The conference will offer many opportunities for networking and discussion.

**Yes**: You'll be meeting colleagues in fun, intimate surroundings, designed to get people talking.

---

When they hatch in late spring, tick larvae are tiny—no bigger than the period at the end of this sentence. Source: http://qz.com/441583/lyme-disease-is-spreading-faster-than-ever-and-humans-are-partly-to-blame/

~~~~~ ~~~~~ ~~~~~

*Make it ugly*

One of my clients uses the term: *make it ugly*. Make it ugly, he says, because *masking reality with mushy text kills impact*. The example above re package-contents ("let's register as a charity!") came from a blog he wrote. Make it ugly instead of making it bland, and your reader will perk up and take notice.

## ~~~~~ Examples ~~~~~

What affected me with the email below is how Annie brought her mother to life so quickly and simply: "just shy of her 42nd birthday" and "funny, smart, caring." There's a reason why charities use stories to raise funds; it works. We can breeze by abstract large numbers about suffering, but we don't do it so well when we can visualize a human being.

*Friends,*

*As many of you know, I lost my mother to cancer many years ago. I was seventeen years old, my mother just shy of her 42nd birthday. I still miss her.*

*If the advancements in treatment had been available then that are here today, my funny, smart, caring Mom could still be alive. So I am really excited about participating in this year's Relay For Life.*

*Please join me in the fight against cancer by supporting my participation in Relay For Life now. It's easy - just click on the link below and you will be directed to my personal donation page.*

*Thanks for your support!*

*Annie*

----

Chip and Dan Heath, revered marketing gurus and authors of *Making it Stick* had a group of students deliver one-minute speeches. The typical student used 2.5 statistics. Only one in ten told a story. Yet when students were asked to *recall* the speeches, nearly two-thirds remembered the stories. Only 5% remembered any individual statistic.

~~~~~ ~~~~~ ~~~~~

| Real-life quote | Bafflegab |
|---|---|
| Just watch me.<br>— *Pierre Trudeau* | Observing demonstrated senior leadership actions will reveal management objectives. |
| Thou shalt not bear false witness against thy neighbor.<br>*Ten Commandments* | If it comes to the attention of Corporate Ethics that an employee has generated materials that have been deemed to be inaccurate in regards to another, formal documented measures will be taken |

|  | by the appropriate officers in order to address and correct misunderstandings. |
|---|---|
| If you're going through hell, keep going.<br><br>— *Winston Churchill* | Obstacles, delays and interventions are an inevitable by-product of the machinations of commercial interactions. To achieve this year's fiscal objectives, consistently apply persistence and a relentless mission focus. |

# 4 Editing is the secret sauce

*Write drunk, edit sober.*

*— Ernest Hemingway*

Think of the last time you heard someone praise someone else's writing ability. Can you remember what they talked about? I'm going to guess that it focused on word wizardry. The ability to turn a phrase, to whip up great prose almost instantly.

Yet no great writer *ever* gained their skill by lobbing paragraphs of perfect polished prose onto the paper. And no great writer *retains* their skill by doing that.

Show me a great writer, and I'll show you a great editor.

## It's a two-part process

Writing is a two-art, two-part process: composition *and* editing. Just like Djokovic or LeBron, every good writer practices. Their entire career. You heard it here first, editing matters **more** than composing. Editing is the secret sauce that turns weak text into strong.

The good news? Editing is a skill like any other. Editing is the gift that keeps on giving. The more you do it, the better you'll be. Forget about learning to compose well. Focus on upping your editing game. It's easier. And you'll get more bang for your buck.

*When something can be read without effort, great effort has gone into its writing*

*— Enrique Jarde Poncela*

*The whole secret of writing is rewriting.*

*— Robert Heinlein, author of Stranger in a Strange Land*

## What is editing, really?

When they think of editing, most people's heads go automatically to the grammar rules of Miss Ledd or the *Chicago Manual of Style*. Forget about them, they're more about proofing than editing.

From now on, think of editing as :

- Pruning your prose
- Moving stuff around to strengthen and clarify your message
- Writing for your reader
- Lather, rinse, repeat.

*A computer programmer had not shown up at his workplace in several days. Nor has he replied to emails or calls. Finally a colleague goes to his house. She finds him in the shower, emaciated and near death. Beside him is an empty bottle of shampoo, with the instructions "Lather, rinse, repeat."*

## Why is everyone still verbose?

Just about everyone complains of other people's writing verbosity. Yet few see their own writing as verbose. It reminds me of a study I read about household environmentalism. The study found that most households feel they are better than average at adhering to sustainable practices. Just about every household also feels that their neighbors are not.

We're not stupid though. So there has to be a reason we're verbose. Over and above the training we got from Miss Ledd, and the tired paradigms of old-school writing.

I have a couple of ideas on that. Actually, four. Four reasons why your editing sucks. I'll share them with you, and once you understand *why* your editing sucks, you'll find it considerably easier to adopt the editing tips and tricks I'll show you.

Let's start by looking at an email that landed in my inbox not too long ago.

~~~~~ **Example** ~~~~~

Pythagorean theorem: 24 words

Lord's prayer: 66 words

Archimedes' Principle: 67 words

Ten Commandments: 179 words

Gettysburg address: 286 words

US Constitution with all 27 Amendments: 7,818

words

EU regulations on the sale of cabbage: 26,911 words

~~~~~ ~~~~~ ~~~~~

*Reason One: Fear*

Fear is a major cause of word-bloat. I can guarantee that the readers of the EU regulations on the sale of cabbage were fearful of not putting everything in. At work, you've often seen people cover their bases by:

- throwing in everything
- qualifying everything.

But doing so detracts from and muddies the business message. You alienate your reader. (You're a chore or a bore? You lose your reader fer shore!)

**Cure: Bravery. Boldness. Don't be afraid to state your message, flat out.**

A good editor (you, as of now) is brave, bold and brutal. Narrowly focused on the message at hand. Brutally cutting out unneeded extras. Yes it's true, those extras *are* related to the topic at hand. Who cares!? Don't include information because it's *related*. Include it because it's *needed*. Right now, right here.

*Reason Two: Trying to do too much*
Communication is a courtship.

More is less.

Let's go with an example to illustrate this one.

~~~~~ **Example** ~~~~~

My client Zoey, a force to be reckoned with, started a business that requires colleges and universities to sign on. When she got on the phone with a new one, she would follow up after the call by sending them an enrolment form, a financial form, a marketing piece, and a FAQ.

But she quickly learned that a) this was overwhelming and b) the various pieces of information weren't getting in front of the right eyes. "Now I just send a link to the enrolment form and the FAQ," she says.

And adds insightfully, "When you do something, you tend to do it in the way that is efficient for you. But it isn't efficient for the recipient. Even though they may need to go through A-Z, your best way of getting them to Z is to first interest them in going through A. Once they've done that, you can talk about the next step."

~~~~~ ~~~~~ ~~~~~

Often, writing fails because **we try to do too much**. Not just within an email as Zoey did, but within each sentence. Within each paragraph.

Have you ever fed a baby in a high chair? If so, who decides on the pace? You, or the baby? Think of business writing as feeding a baby. Stuffing in fat fistfuls of information won't work. The baby (your reader) will move its head aside, close its mouth, spit things out – you know the drill. The baby – your reader – sets the pace.

**Cure:** Hone in narrowly on your goal. Coldly cut out whatever doesn't move your reader towards *that specific goal*. Then cut more. You may need 100 words or 1,000 or 10,000 or 100,000; that depends on the medium and the format. The point is, you want to delete extraneous facts that could be delivered in another message. You want your reader to read; you want them to understand. Focus on the essence, jettison the rest.

More is less.

~~~~~ **Example** ~~~~~

My friend JohnG, a man with an astonishing memory for details, is a lawyer. JohnG used to send out emails to his clients that asked a number of sequential questions, because he's the kind of guy that can and does answer such emails efficiently.

Then he and I had a discussion about the responses he was getting ("They're driving me crazy, Marcia! I send them an email with five questions and they write back and say "Yes!""). Now he sends emails that include only one or two questions. Once he has his answer, John goes on to the next issue. Sounds cumbersome? Actually, it saves time.

~~~~~ ~~~~~ ~~~~~

*Reason Three: Being too precise*

*Precise* is not a good thing, in and of itself. Precise is a *relative* term. You need to be just precise enough for the needs of the message today. **Not** as precise as is possible, or as precise as you'd be in a legal document. *Precise* gets in the way of readability.

Everyone gets "Thou shalt not steal." Now, if

you were composing the Security and Exchange rules for the New York Stock Exchange, you'd have to be more precise than that. But in your daily writing at work, you're probably not composing rules for the NYSE.

Chances are, you're often too precise. Be only as precise as you need to be, because precision takes up a lot of words, and every time you use a lot of words you drive your reader away.

**Cure:** Remind yourself as you edit that you pay in lost attention for what you gain with greater precision. Don't keep text in because it is correct. Keep it in because you need it.

### Reason Four: Ego
Every writer falls in love with their words, the second they hit the page. Deleting hurts. Trust me, I feel your pain, I live it every day. As William Faulkner noted, writers have to kill their darlings.

Ego is the reason everyone finds it easier to pare down someone else's text than their own. Following, a few ways to distance yourself from your words and become a better editor ;-). Pick one, try it out. Then try another.

## Edit everything

Edit every single thing you write. Without exception.

Plan to spend about 60-90% (dependent upon format) of your writing time in composing, 10-40% in editing. For a 60-second email, use about 45 seconds to compose and 15 for a review/edit. The longer the piece you're writing, the greater percentage of time invested will be in editing. For example, if it's a book about how to write to get things done at work, plan to spend about 50% or more of your time editing <sigh>.

The difficulty of deleting your own words will never vanish – I often find myself making a slew of edits to a paragraph before I face up to the harsh reality that the world can live without it. I hate it when that happens.

Patience grasshopper! It takes a while to change your mindset. But the more you edit, the better and faster you will become. You'll make huge improvements soon, and more over time.

And as you read further you'll learn time-saving tricks that help you avoid writer's block and allow you to free-write. These will free up writing time for editing.

~~~~~ **Example** ~~~~~

(every little bit helps)

**No**: The data was there for retrospective purposes, not for proactive purposes.

**Yes**: The data was there for retrospective purposes, not proactive.

~~~~~ ~~~~~ ~~~~~

# Four tricks to help you edit better

*Trick One: Make a copy*

Say you've written a first draft of a document called *New employee overview*. Save it and make a copy called: *New employee overview v1*.

In *New employee overview v1*, delete viciously. Attack like a jackal on steroids. Whittle to the bone, then whittle more. Remember, you've preserved all your precious babies in the original file – you can always retrieve them later.

You'll find you never do, but it's startling how much it frees your spirit to know that you can. Having that copy sets free the Inner Slasher that rises up when you edit other people's documents. And you always want to nurture your Inner Slasher.

### Trick Two: The long good-bye

Cut the phrase, sentence, para or section that you suspect should probably go, but are having trouble parting with. Paste it to the end of your document (ideally, with a page break preceding). I call this technique *the long good-bye*.

Once you've finished the document, you'll find you've moved on. The grieving is done. You'll have surprisingly little difficulty deleting your once-treasured text-bits.

### Trick Three: Build a text treasure trove

Maintain a separate Word doc of things you've deleted from other docs. That way you'll always have the nuggets on hand: your own personal data bank of great writing. Your best lines, your favorite ideas. The occasion will come when you will want to use what you have deleted, and you'll have it right there at the ready.

## *Trick Four: Play editing games*

**Figure 1 How do you get to Carnegie Hall? Practice practice practice...**

Here are a couple of head-games to play.

*Editing game 1, Imagine a Penalty*   You work for Minstrel Toothshine, a forward-looking firm with a reverence for concise writing. At Minstrel Toothshine, every desk-job employee gets a hefty writing bonus in their weekly paycheck.

But there's a catch. For every single word you write on the job, necessary or not, you lose a dollar from the bonus. Every week, your writing bonus is decreased by the appropriate total amount. The idea is that you will still write, but you will only write words that are necessary. Minstrel Toothshine *wants* you to write words that are necessary – hence the bonus – but *only* those words – hence the penalty.

69

Now, keep that penalty in mind whenever you write *anything* in your job. Say to yourself, is this *word* worth a dollar to me / my job / my career? And is this *sentence* worth $15.00? Is this *paragraph* worth $150.00?

Remember, those dollars add up.

*Editing game 2, Imagine a Reward* This is the inverse of the same game. Imagine you get a $1 reward for every word you cut from any work-related document or email you send.

### Trick Five: Pretend you're someone else

This is the most powerful trick, bar none. Have you ever noticed that many people can edit other's work, but not their own? The more you can distance yourself from your work, the better editor you will be. More importantly, the better writer you will be. And the better communicator and professional.

You can go further and recruit an editing buddy at work. Agree that you will each, as needed, serve the other as a reviewer/editor of documents. Here's a funny thing – you'll find that you will edit yourself better when you know your friend is going to review a document. Just like the person who cleans their house before the cleaning lady comes.

## You're already playing these silly games

By the way ... you are already playing these silly games at work.

You are *already* getting docked $1 every time you write an extra word – in terms of hurting your personal brand. Every time you are not clear, or you waste people's time, you damage your rep.

Conversely, you buff it up every time you communicate effectively. Every time you are brief and to-the-point, you shine up your personal brand.

I can see you right now, by the way. Yelling at me with your eyes that your manager's writing is verbose and hard to follow. Agreed, it probably is. But they got that position *in spite of* that writing. Not because of it.

Many organizational studies have correlated excellent internal communication to increased profitability. I kid you not. Leaders who communicate well are a tremendous asset to their organizations.

## Now the good news: editing makes your writing life easier

It's **much** easier to be clear and get your point across if you cut down on sentence and paragraph length. Train yourself to:

- Cut out unneeded sections or chapters.

- Cut out extra paragraphs.

- Cut out extra sentences.

- Cut out extra words.

And by the way, you do **not** have to do it in this order. I rarely do. But once you pare your document down, you'll find you can **see** it better. You can work with it better. You can move stuff around. You can begin to dance.

This is particularly true for short paragraphs – once you start shortening your paragraphs, you'll notice how much easier it is to work with them.

Do you know the scene in *Rainman* when Cruise is teaching his autistic brother (Hoffman) to dance? And Hoffman is moving like a tailor's dummy? (If you haven't seen this, you've missed a classic.) You can't dance, you can't be fluid, when everything is bulky and stiff.

**You can move sentences around**, shake things up, and see where you want to go, when your paras and sentences are short. And – bonus – you'll find that when you shorten your sentences and cut down on your verbiage, you'll decrease your use of the passive voice (more on that later).

Cut and rejoin your sentences in new ways that work better. You're using a word processor, not pencil-and-paper – take advantage! It's faster to write a series of short sentences and then work with them. Leave some as they are; join some to others when it suits.

## Editing tip: find the salient sentence

Let's say you've written the first draft of a 1-2 page document. And now you're in edit mode. First step? Look for the most powerful sentence. The one that says what you want to say.

Now, *move* that sentence. Make it the first sentence of your first paragraph. Bring the whole paragraph with it, if it helps. But **start with that strong sentence**. Not with a whole pile of explanatory bumf. The bumf can go later. Better yet, you may be able to delete it.

~~~~~ **Example** ~~~~~

A sales trainer had written a blog about her sales process with new prospects. The first line of the blog was *Much of the work I do with new prospects is to help them identify and clarify their sales process*. But it wasn't until four (4!) paragraphs later, that she finally got back to her opening sentence – which had been the entire point of her blog post.

In a coaching session, I showed her how to take the four-paras-too-late section and move it to the start, after this 11-word intro: *Here's what I do after the first meeting with a prospect.* Instantly the blog became punchier, clearer, stronger. Show don't tell! And get to the point!

~~~~~ ~~~~~ ~~~~~

Now, try swapping your sentences around in other places. Move the first sentence in a paragraph to the end. How does that look? Feel?

Cut a sentence into two, making whatever minor revisions that requires. Does that clarify? Add pace / interest?

Playing with sentences and looking at the results

works better than thinking. It's faster too. And less painful. In other words, don't over-analyze. Just use trial-and-error. Try out a few sentence swaps, see how they look. Keep moving.

*Paragraph breaks – revisited*

Try moving paragraph breaks around as you edit. Throw a new paragraph break into a longer para to cut it into two. (Note that you don't have to put the cut in the exact middle of the long paragraph – be creative!)

How does that look? Like it? Not?

All this can be the work of a few seconds or minutes. Changing where you break for a new paragraph is a powerful easy trick to make your writing more engaging.

# Dealing with context

Business writing tends to provide too much context or too little. Beware both pitfalls!

*Where you are in your document* provides the key to appropriate context. Your reader is most likely to need context at the beginning. They need to know:

1. Why you are writing this
2. Why they should care
3. What action you are looking for
4. Any **necessary** backstory

*Too little context – it happens at the beginning*
The too-little-context writer assumes you know all the facts and back story, and care as much as they do about the topic. But of course you don't. And you won't, without context.

You'll never go wrong by making it clear to your business reader, at the outset:

1. Why they should care
2. What action you're looking for.

One style-trick is to provide that context in an italicized intro, as in the example below. The italics are a heads-up to your reader that this part is context. Once you go back to non-italics, they know the intro is over.

~~~~~ **Example** ~~~~~

*In the month of May, Bernanke and his top advisors met four times to discuss quantitative easing. While no decision appears to have been reached, Bernanke appears to be softening his stance.*

Bernanke's ability to stop the flow of [article continues...]

~~~~~ ~~~~~ ~~~~~

*Too* much *context – it happens in the middle*
*Once you have established your topic,* you can cut down on verbiage. Most writers forget this. They establish at the outset what they're talking about, and then fail to cut back later on.

~~~~~ Examples ~~~~~

Recently I was writing a piece on team building. Once the reader knew I was on this topic, I no longer had to use the term *team* before *member* or *building* – I could just use *member* or *building*. Similarly, *new HR career-planning program* can be referred to, mid- or late-document, as *the program. Scalable analysis and delivery process* can be referred to as *the process.*

**Action**: Get into the habit of checking your writing to see if you continue to use the bulky phrasing that was needed at the outset. You'll be astonished at what a difference this makes!

---

Your contact information should be part of your primary navigation so visitors can find it regardless of where they are ~~on your site~~.

---

Our ~~main~~ objective is to communicate, not to decorate. Our designs ~~solutions~~ are ~~always~~ functional and effective.

---

When someone offers you free advice and they have done what you are trying to do, pay attention ~~to them~~. You could be just as successful ~~as them~~!

~~~~~ ~~~~~ ~~~~~

*Problem-based learning – it's up to you!*
Problem-based learning (PBL) was developed at McMaster Medical School in Canada in the 60s and has since caught on around the globe. It was developed by staff members who felt that memorizing massive amounts of medical facts was not delivering the results they wanted. So instead, they set problems for the students, early

on in their medical training. The students then had to find out what information they needed and work together to apply it. With PBL, students learn through solving problems.

I'm presenting editing to you as a type of problem-based learning. If you accept my premise that every extra word hurts you – every single one – you will teach yourself to get better and better at writing concisely. If you don't accept the premise, you won't.

You're a smart person. I don't have to tell you how to cut out words, which words to cut out, or when. You just have to decide that you want to.

# 5. Beating writer's block

*Writing is easy – just open a vein.*

*— Quoted so often that we don't know who said it first*

*I don't have writer's block. I have writer's blockage.*

*— Fran Lebowitz*

*Writing is easy. Get out a piece of paper. Write the word 'the.' Stare at it for four hours. Add 'hell with it' and move on.*

*— Heard on CBC Radio*

## Everyone's nemesis

**Everyone** gets writer's block, **all the time**. Not just the pros. Writing is a horrid, deeply unnatural act.

Writing forces us to put our words out blindly, to an unseen audience. And be judged.

When we speak, we can look for reactions. By verbal and facial clues, we know if our listeners understand. At any point in our message their reactions show us how and when to modify our course.

But with writing! We must express our thoughts without being there to watch our listener and change tack when necessary. We have to make so many choices when we write, without benefit of listener feedback. It's difficult to decide, at every fork in the road, which choice is smartest and best. And once we do choose, another one rears its ugly head. Writing is the classic nightmare of presenting naked to a large audience.

## Smart peoples writes good!

Worst of all, many of us feel, whether or not we realize it, that *writing is the ultimate expression of our intelligence and education.* Ouch! Ouch ouch!

Besides the pain and irritation (I know, I'm sounding like a hemorrhoid commercial here, bear with me), writer's block is a terrific waste of time. A big impediment to efficiency.

And it's a chronic, incurable condition. But there are ways to battle it. Following, a few approaches and tips. (For the hemorrhoids, you're on your own.)

## Free writing, aka BARF!

**Free writing** is a wondrous, proven, powerful way to break through writing resistance. Writing expert Peter Elbow discusses free writing in depth in *Writing with Power* and *Writing Without Teachers.* Anne Handley recommends that you "show up and throw up" in her book on creating business content. Writer Anne Lamott uses the term Shitty First Draft: "*All good writers write them. This is how they end up with good second drafts and terrific third drafts.*"

Just … write.

Keep writing.

Put *anything* down on the page.

Did I say, keep writing?

Don't listen if your inner critic whines at you in *that* voice: "Why start – it will be crappy. People will laugh. And there's a far far better way to write this if only you could think of it."

My name for free writing is the Blow Away Restrictions – Flow! (BARF) approach. Don't think. Don't criticize yourself. Throw whatever you're thinking about onto the page. Upchuck.

Always remember, you're writing virtually. On paper that doesn't exist, with ink that hasn't been used yet. Later, you can move things around, delete, and re-work. That part is easy.

So don't hold back. Get moving. BARF freely. Time is the scarcest resource.

## Other ways to wrestle writer's block

*Pomodoro et al*

Pomodoro is a fun little app that helps you snip your writing moments into tiny slices (http://www.pomodorotechnique.com/timer/).

Open your document and tell yourself you only have to write for 15 minutes. Get moving. Throw down any sentences, ideas, or paras you can during that time. Do not edit. If possible, do not think.

If you're lucky, you'll get in the groove and keep working. If not, you'll have 15 minutes writing done. The point is to break it down, reduce the torture. Make the exit sign clearly visible and not too far away. Do **not** worry about quality or organization. Just get your paws on the keyboard. Do not answer the phone / check emails / whatever. You'll be surprised when the bell rings!

### Talker's block
Write like you talk. As business/Internet rock star Seth Godin says, no one ever gets talker's block. By the way, when I say *write* here, I mean *compose*. *Compose* like you talk. Edit later.

### Feel free to fail
Beating your head against a brick wall as you try to get perfection on a first draft is an *extremely* poor use of your time. Yet we've all done it.

Give yourself permission to fail! You'll get going faster, save time, and the end result will be stronger.

*Put yourself on the analyst couch*

Ask yourself "What's blocking me?" Spend a short time thinking up your answer and then try to get your ideas down on paper. Don't worry too much if these words won't be useable in your document; at the least they'll help unblock and get you started.

*Word splattering – aka word processor thinking*

Most of us formed our first letters with a physical tool on a physical surface. Not a virtual one. Say a crayon, on paper. Which means that you, poor vestige from the non-virtual age, saw and learned writing as a *linear*, physical task.

apple
lemon
banana

By the time you were ten you wondered how to start and where you would go next. Almost always, you were writing for a teacher who would grade what you wrote. Reading every word, looking for errors.

*Let's play an imagination game...*

You've just woken up. Stumbled into the bathroom. As you stare at the mirror above the sink an inspiration lights up the foggy recesses of your brain.

You write with a word processor! Not pen and paper.

Scrawl that thought on your imaginary bathroom mirror. Use a sharpie or lipstick. Blood red.

Now you're looking at something like this:

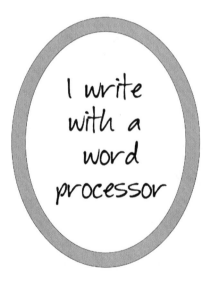

Why did we just play that game? To get you thinking about the difference between composing with physical tools (your *childhood* experience) and writing digitally (your *today* experience).

Writing digitally, you can flee the linear:

- Start your writing piece anywhere!

- Start in the middle of your progress report.

- Start with the part you're excited about.

- Start with the conclusion.

- It doesn't matter. Get words down! Move stuff around afterwards.

## Plan a reward

Do you typically stop for coffee or tea or water mid-morning? Perfect. Around ten a.m., tell yourself that you'll work for 15-20 minutes on a writing job before your break. The break is the reward – no 15-20 minutes composing, no break.

## Chop chop!

Chop up your writing work. Here are two ways:

1. Plan several short writing sessions, say four 15-minute writing sessions in a day. 4 x 15 is, I think, 60, which makes – oh boy! – an hour. In which time you can accomplish quite a bit.

2. Work on two or three writing tasks at once. Hop from one to the next whenever you get stuck.

*Start by imagining you're explaining to a friend*
Imagine you're *telling* a friend or colleague what you need to say in this document. Spend a minute or three doing that in your head. Then get your head down and start hitting keys.

*Write a letter to a friend. Or yourself. Or your mom.*
As above, but actually do it. Let's say it's a two-page report on whether to proceed with a new RFP. Start writing. First, pretend you're giving a quick intro to the friend. Don't worry about format or flow. Just describe to your friend the nature of the issue and a few of the deciding factors.

Now, throw a bit of format at it. Put in a few simple headers. Take some of the sentences or paras you've written and place them where they belong. See? You're already halfway done.

*Back-of-an-envelope – or write out some questions*
*Full disclosure* Making a written outline intimidates me. Both creating and adhering to one. I tend to

outline in my head. Then write. Then move sections about once I see what I've got. I create structure after the fact – in fact I create structure by writing.

This is not true for many. And no question, getting going is really a matter of breaking things down, de-magnifying the task.

Outlines can help with that. Outlines can break it down, turn a challenging assignment into a bunch of less-daunting bits. Then you can write a few words on one of the little bits, and then a few more, and so on. If a detailed outline works for you, create and use one.

Alternatively, write down a few questions your reader might want you to answer. Start answering one of them, then move to the next.

### Use software to chunk it up

I used Scrivener for the early stages of this book. It's a lovely piece of software that provides many tools to break any writing project into chunks. In theory, you can do this with Word, but in practice Scrivener has considerable advantages. It's particularly strong at presenting your book visually, in a way that's easy to take in and work with. If you are working on a long document, take a look at tools like Scrivener that might help you.

### Ditch the distractions!

Many pieces of writing software – including Word and Scrivener – have an option called *writer's format* or *full screen*. This view removes visual distractions from your monitor. You see only the piece you're working on and almost nothing else – no menu bars or other such distractions. I didn't like it at first, but I've come around to it. It's calming.

# 6. Divide and Conquer

The next step is to divide and conquer – to *separate* composing from editing.

Composing and editing simultaneously is a self-defeating practice. It hamstrings progress. And wastes time. It frustrates, discourages, and drums in our dislike of writing.

Performers (athletes, musicians, actors) take a different approach. They are in *practice* OR *performance* mode.

**Practice mode** In *practice* mode, performers work to hone their technique. They take note of where their feet are, their hands, their head, how they move, how it sounds. They try new approaches.

They criticize themselves. They listen to coaches.

**Performance mode** On The Big Day – the match, the opening night, the concert – they move into *performance* mode ... they let everything execute unconsciously. Those who can do this best tend to perform best.

*Composing* is akin to performance mode. In performance mode, get out of your own way. Don't criticize. Shut up your silly head. Write down anything. Let it flow!

*Editing* then, is practice mode. Look at what you've done. Mess with it. Fix it. Make it better.

## Learn to be in editing OR composing mode. Not both.

Does this sound familiar? You:

1. Dread any writing job, particularly the start.

2. Postpone.

3. Re-postpone.

4. Finally open a Word doc. Stare at a blank page.

5. Begin to put words down. Scratch out, rethink, sweat.

6. Berate yourself. Stop and start a couple more times.

7. Move to a lower-pain activity.

When you choose to write in both editing and composing mode? You are, in effect, standing behind your own shoulder and heckling yourself as you try to perform.

But guess what? You can't suck and blow at the same time.

Imagine:

- Playing a sport
- Negotiating a deal
- Kissing

...while you stand behind your own shoulder and carp at your performance.

Recently, while explaining this practicing-versus-performing concept to Zoey, I used this standing-behind-your-own-shoulder metaphor.

She replied, "Marcia, I live my whole life that way."

Zoey is an amazing woman. But please, do not try to emulate this aspect of her character.

## The first step is awareness

As with so many problems, the first step is awareness, admitting, taking ownership. You know, you stand up and say ... *My name is [...] and I am an edit-while-composing-aholic.*

Here are three steps to try:

1. Be aware of which mode you are in.

2. Be in one or the other. Not both. Be BARFing or editing.

3. Go easy, nurse yourself when you are in BARF (composing) mode. Let yourself be the awkwardest writer ever. Clumsy phrasing, the wrong word, it doesn't matter.

Think of your first draft as your half-painted room. Masking tape everywhere, try-out strokes randomly on walls, an abandoned ladder, plate-less light switches. This is **not** for public consumption. This part can look like a dog's breakfast. In fact, it's better if it does.

## The pause that refreshes

One of the best things you can do, post-BARF, is to take a break. Move on to something else. You'll find when you come back that your subconscious has done a lot of work for you.

As time goes by, you'll improve at switching from editing to composition mode. Particularly if you just remind yourself of which mode you are in, and get off your own case when it's free-writing mode. Oddly enough, by the way, you don't tend to berate yourself in editing mode! Only in composition.

# How perfectionism gets in your way

You do **not** have to be a perfectionist to fall into perfectionist behavior. There are many ways to be a perfectionist.

*Don't let* excellent *be the enemy of* good

*A good plan violently executed now is better than a perfect plan executed next week.*

*— George S. Patton*

When my friend Emer was working on her thesis she was given a piece of great advice:

*The only good thesis is a published thesis.*

aka

*Done is better than perfect*

*— Mark Zuckerberg*

Despite this, Emer, like most thesis-starters, didn't finish. Her thesis has languished in a dusty corner of her house/head for decades.

## Satisficing versus maximizing

Are you a maximizer or a satisficer? Maximizers are perfectionists; they want to make the absolute best choice. Satisficers find a good-enough solution, and move on.

If you're a maximizer, you'll find it harder to go into free-wheeling free-writing mode. If so, keep telling yourself that at the start, poor writing *is* the best route, it *is* maximizing, it's the first step to a great outcome.

### The ugly intersection of writing and perfectionism

If you'd like to read more on the intersection of writing and perfectionism, check out the post by Kathy Gottberg of smartliving365.com, in the Resources section of wyws.ca. Here's a quote Kathy includes, from Anne Lamott, whom you may remember from the BARF section earlier on:

*"Perfectionism is the voice of the oppressor, the enemy of the people. It will keep you cramped and insane your whole life, and it is the main obstacle between you and a shitty first draft."*

# 7. Hearing the other guy's head

*Don't Make Me Think!* is the title of one of the most successful web design books ever. It still sells, although it was published in 2000. The title is a great motto for website design.

It's an equally great motto for writing at work. You want to make it easy for your reader to follow your argument. You do **not** want to make them think or struggle to follow you. Your reader is bombarded with things-to-read. Your reader is busy and impatient. Your reader has a digital [read 'short'] attention span.

Which means you need to put yourself into your reader's head. Or shoes.

There's irony for you – the more you base your message on how *you* think, feel, act, and want, the more likely it is that you *won't* get what you want.

Why is it so hard to get into your reader's head? Because you live, 24/7, in your *own* head.

## The curse of knowledge

Worse yet, whatever you're writing about, you know too well. You repeatedly *over*estimate your readers' ability to follow what you say, because you just can't help thinking that they know your subject/topic as well as you do. This phenomenon is called the *curse of knowledge* (Google it!).

Steven Pinker writes about the *curse of knowledge* in his book, *The Sense of Style*. It's one of the reasons why manuals are hard to understand: the person writing the manual can no longer remember what it was like to *not* understand the thing they are writing about. It's why the best teachers or coaches of any given skill (carpentry, tennis, engineering) are not usually the best *practitioners,* they're the best *communicators.* They can get outside their own heads.

When you're speaking, it's much easier. Your listener gives you feedback with facial expressions: nods, shakes, interruptions and questions. When your communication car veers onto an unpaved shoulder, you can backtrack, take a new route, try again.

With writing, not so much. You and your reader exist in separate parts of the time-space continuum. No feedback, or at least no feedback until afterwards.

## Gondola Gondola

I'm what Malcolm Gladwell has termed an early adopter; I get all fired up by new ideas.

In the paper one morning I heard about a brilliant solution to the knotty problem of transporting people to our downtown airport in Toronto. And why is this such a problem? Because the downtown airport is on an island, separated from the mainland by a worrisome 200-yard width of water.

At the time, travelers to the island airport had to take a ferry. But the ferry added a whole new level of complexity to air travel – travellers had to time

the ferry departure to catch their plane –
significantly increasing travel time, complexity,
and bother.

Saturday morning, after a doubles squash game, I
told my friends all about the new idea.

"Some urban planner has come up with an
amazing transit idea," I told them. "Using
gondolas for getting over to the island airport! He
says they use them in Portland. And in Rio. And
he thinks we could too. They have waaay more
capacity than you might guess. And they're cheap.
And totally eco. And they're a killer tourist
attraction."

Out of the corner of my eye, I half-noticed that
my friend Lynn, unlike the other two, wasn't
nodding or smiling. She didn't look disapproving.
Just a bit … perplexed.

"I love that idea!" Dorothy said.

"Me too," said Cheryl. "Is there any chance it could happen?"

Lynn spoke up before I could reply. "Wouldn't they be cold?"

"Cold?" said Dorothy. "Cold? I mean, they're made for winter. Don't they have heaters?"

"Heaters?" said Lynn. "A heater, in a gondola? Are you serious? Wouldn't that be dangerous? And isn't the lake waaay too deep? You are joking about this Marce, right?"

Light finally dawned. *Lynn* was thinking of a narrow Venetian boat. *I* was talking about an aerial lift.

We still laugh about that. Imagining the shivering tourists, baggage piled precariously in narrow open boats. Or the new Canadians, wide-eyed as they work their way through the queue, buffaloed by this crazy-canuck process.

Not to mention the stalwart gondoliers, navigating the semi-frozen waters on frigid February days.

*If the gondola concept interests you, please head to wyws.ca/resources for more information.*

## We write from our own viewpoint

While I told my story? I *knew* I was talking about an aerial lift. I could see the gondolas in my head. I still can. We communicate from our own viewpoint. But Lynn was seeing and hearing a whole different picture.

## Why it's hard to hear the other guy's head

Communication ... is what the other person thinks you said.

Every reader comes to you with a mindset in place, a predisposition, a set of assumptions. Not only that, they're busy at work, they have a ton of other things going on. They're distracted, only half paying attention to what you wrote.

If our point isn't clear when we *speak*, if our listener can't follow, they tell us in a million different ways, using words, facial gestures, and motions. We're so used to this that we automatically adjust as we see the effect of our words on our listener.

**But! With writing it's different.** There's that

wall of space and time between us and our writer. What *we* carefully explain, our *reader* may already understand, and skim over in irritation. And what we fail to clarify may mystify.

**Internal leaps** Did you make any internal leaps that your reader won't follow? Are you writing about what **you** plan to do/achieve? Or are you putting yourself in the reader's place, explaining what **they** need to do/know/achieve?

**Mood / Tone / Audience** Don't forget mood and tone (particularly in emails)! If someone feels an angry tone of voice they will interpret the content entirely differently than if they had visualized you smiling.

*Five steps to hearing the other guy's head*

Awareness
The first step is awareness (isn't it always...). *Know* that your head and your reader's will be out of alignment. Expect it. Be aware of it, **every time you write anything**. Earth to you ... ding ding ding ... could your message be misinterpreted? Read it again! Train yourself to read with an other-minded eye. Do it every time, and you'll improve at it, fast.

## Identify the goal - WIIFM

Start by identifying the goal of your message. Tell them *why* they want to read what you have written. At the outset, answer the eternal internal question of anyone at a desk: *What's in it for me (WIIFM)?*

## Identify your audience

Think about who your audience is. What they know already. And what they need to know. (Not necessarily the same as what you want to tell them.)

Identifying your audience helps you focus on their needs and interests. Try to think of **a specific person** who will be reading what you wrote. This is similar to the buyer persona concept used in marketing – we reach our audience better when we feel we're writing to a specific, real human being. Corporate-speak often does the opposite, and it blows by us unheard.

## Distance training

Train yourself to *pull away* from what you've written. Think – could a reader, particularly a hasty, careless reader – misunderstand it? Try to read what you've written as a distracted reader. Someone who does not make the intuitive leaps you do (because you know what you're writing about). Use connecting words, and pull your reader along by the nose.

~~~~~ *Example* ~~~~~

I often buy things online from a place I'll call Clearly Glasses. A couple of months ago an email with the subject *"Don't Forget to Vote, Clearly Fans!"* landed in my inbox.

I thought *fans*? Huh? Does Clearly Glasses sell fans? And why am I voting on the fans? I've never bought one! And what kind of fans are *Clearly* fans? Or am I supposed to be *voting* clearly?

Turns out, Clearly Glasses was asking me to vote for them in a contest – they were finalists for an e-commerce innovation award. They wanted my support (which they got, once I deciphered their email, because they have great products, prices and service).

~~~~~ ~~~~~ ~~~~~

Here's a tip – once you complete a rough draft that's of any consequence:

1. Print it

2. Read it aloud. Or pretend you're doing so, if you're not alone.

Leaps that leave the reader behind will become much more evident. Breaks in flow or logic are more visible. Try it!

~~~~~ *Example* ~~~~~

Giving directions with inadequate direction

In pre-cellphone days, a neighbor gave me directions to his lakeside home in Prince Edward County. Technically, they were correct. They started with:

Take the first two right turns after leaving highway 401 at exit 395.

But he neglected to mention that while the *first* right turn was 1 mile after getting off the highway, the *second* one was 21 miles further on! I spent the entire 21 miles thinking I'd missed the second turn-off. Havering and fussing to myself, in the dark.

Most people provide terrible directions. They suffer from the Curse of Knowledge. They cannot remember what it was like to navigate the route when they first encountered it. If you can provide good written directions, give yourself a pat on the back. You're a communicator.

~~~~~ ~~~~~ ~~~~~

# The easiest tip ever

Go heavy on the word *you*. Start sentences with *you*.

You'll find It makes an astonishing difference.

You heard it here first.

# Structure and organization

*The past, the present, and the future walked into a bar. It was tense.*

I won't tell you how to organize your writing in this book; it's beyond the scope. I will give you just a few ideas to ponder.

**Some of us like** to organize before we start to write, some as we compose, some afterwards. No question, the longer the document, the more upfront organizing you will need to do. But all of these can work, including a combination of two or three.

**Organize before**: Here's the one you learned in school. Before you start, you create an outline of your document, in the order that you will present it (but today, not necessarily in the order that you will write it – remember, you write virtually, with a word processor). If you're like me and don't enjoy organizing, set yourself free with this one – make the outline rough; write it on the back of an envelope; and/or spend very little time on this task. You can get back to it later.

**Organize during**: You start with any section or sentence, and as you move on to the next one you start moving pieces and sentences around.

**Organize after**: You have already done some *organizing during*, but now you really get down to your task. You say to yourself: could this whole section be moved to the back? Or the front? What would that do? Same with sentences. Get creative!

I use all three types of organization, although, as mentioned, the amount of upfront organizing I do increases with the length of the document I'm working on. I find that over-focusing on organization sets off writer's block. If you're stuck, start writing about whatever is easiest or most interesting. Go from there.

~~~~~ **Example** ~~~~~

Recently I heard Wally Lamb (if you enjoy reading fiction and haven't met up with Wally yet, you're in for a treat) interviewed on radio. The host said: *Wally, you do a number of things that are intriguing in your latest book. Particularly the multi-voice narration, with 8 voices heard in alternating chapters. Why did you pick that technique?*

Wally: Well Michael, your question presupposes that I have a game plan. And I don't.

~~~~~ ~~~~~ ~~~~~

## Organization checklist – can your document fly on its own?

Here's what you want to think about before you click *send* or push any verbal fledgling out of the nest:

**Context** Have you provided context at the start? Can your reader see, near-instantly, why you're writing and what's-in-it-for-me?

**Reader-view** Is your document organized in terms of what you see/think/feel, or is it organized in terms of what the reader wants to know? Yes, organizational templates affect this. But still, keep your reader's needs in mind.

**Headers and sub-headers** Remember to use headers and sub-headers **liberally**. In minutes, in reports, in blog posts. Even in emails! Remember? We're shedding the old paradigms, they're decades out of date. **You can use headers whenever you please**. You do not have to be writing up your chemistry lab report to use headers.

**Check your assumptions!** The pace of work today often results in hasty start-up of any given task. *Before* you start on a time-consuming document, consider sending this to your manager: *As I understand it, you are looking for a one-page summary of the main points of the ABC proposal by August 27, including estimates of the costs for each section and projected delivery dates. Please let me know by DATE if this is what you'd like to see.*

**Start with your main point** *You buried the lead!* is an invective often hurled at junior journalists. Put the lead – your critical message – upfront and center! Identify that critical sentence or paragraph – it's in there, somewhere! – and pull it to the top. In an email, use it as the subject line.

If your lead lurks unseen in the middle of an email/letter/proposal/presentation, your reader may not give it its due. Unconsciously they think, *it's in the middle of the 4th paragraph – it's not important.*

# 8. Advanced tips and a wee sprinkling of grammar

*Outside of a dog, a book is a man's best friend. Inside of a dog, it's too dark to read.*

*— Groucho Marx*

## You can relax now

We've discussed composition and editing and writer's block. Plus getting into your reader's head. What follows are a few tips to help you build on that foundation.

## Always write scannable text. No exceptions.

You might be thinking: why should I write

*scannable* text? I want my reader to *read*, not scan!

Meet Jakob Nielsen, a world-renowned web usability consultant whose oft-cited study about reading on the web revealed that ... people don't actually do it. Instead, they scan, picking out words and bits of interest. A whopping 79% *always* scan any new page they came across; only 16% read word-by-word.

You may now be arguing that you aren't writing for the web. But I hear your voice getting smaller. Orange is the new black; scanning is the new reading.

The good news – writing scannable text makes it *more* likely that your reader will read. It's inviting! It offers generous white space, headers that guide and clarify, and none of those bulky blocky paragraphs. Scannable text:

- Is humble, considerate, and reader-focused
- Respects your reader's tight schedule, their need to zone in on main points, and the possibility that they will need to view your message more than once.

Scannable text **puts control in the hands of the reader**. Your reader can read in the way that suits the moment, such as:

- Initial once-over

- Careful review

- Quick catch-up before a meeting.

What makes your text scannable? You're well on your way if you:

1. Begin by stating your main point and why readers want/need to hear it.

2. Use short words, sentences and paragraphs.

3. Use *meaningful* headers throughout (not descriptive labels, such as *Observations*). Your *meaningful* headers, read in sequence, should give an outline of the document.

4. Use **boldface** and *italics* to highlight important points and calls-to-action.

5. And of course, edit ruthlessly.

## Dummy's guide to passive-active

Eek! That wretched active-passive thing!

You've probably run into the misery of active-passive voice? Maybe, in a writing workshop, where you half-listened to the instructor?

If so, let's flash-forward to three days later. You're motoring through the office kitchen, grabbing a green tea before heading back to your desk. But a fellow workshop attendee, plucking a triple-zero yogurt from the bar fridge, bars your path. She has a question for you.

*You were at that workshop on Tuesday weren't you, the writing one?*

*Mmm ... yes.*

*You know that thing about active and passive voice? ...Did you get it?*

You open your mouth to answer. Stop.

Stare at her blankly, the just-filched maple-glazed from the planning meeting arrested halfway between hand and mouth.

Terms like *subject, object,* and *verb to be* stumble about in your skull. Bearing down, you can almost recall fragments of those highly recommended active-voice sentences – maybe about half of each one. You do remember that passive was bad. *Active*, the instructor said, focusing her gimlet eye directly on you, *is shorter and livelier.*

You lift your eyes to the yogurt questioner.

"No," you say.

## *You only need to learn three little clues*

But you *don't* have to get it. You just have to learn *three little clues*. Three flags to alert you to the passive voice in your writing.

Once you recognize the nasty little rodent, you have a better chance of stomping it out (this didn't work with rabbits in Australia, but I digress. Oh! Guess what I learned today? Rabbits are not rodents! They're lagomorphs. No, I don't really know what a lagomorph is. Besides, this is a book about writing. Try to stay on topic.)

The three little clues:

1. Active voice typically uses the first person: *I* or *we*.

2. Passive has no *I* or *we*, but often uses *by*.

3. Passive typically bulks up its verbs by pulling in parts of the verb *to be* (is, was, will, to be … for examples see the Wordle that follows).

**Figure 2 Examples of passive wording**

## ~~~~~ Examples ~~~~~

Passive: This issue will **be** addressed **by** the dictatorship at the next convention.

Active: We will address this issue at the next convention.

Passive: It **was** decided **by** the steering committee that the report needed revision.

Active: The steering committee decided that the report needed revision.

Passive: The Pinot Grigio **was** hoovered up **by** the steering committee.

Active: The steering committee hoovered up the Pinot Grigio.

~~~~~ ~~~~~ ~~~~~

## Why is passive frowned upon?

Here are a few reasons why passive is often (not always) a poor choice:

- By keeping the identity of the subject secret, it feels evasive.

- *Passive*: Mistakes were found during the audit, and steps have been taken to correct them.

- *Active*: We found mistakes during the audit and I have taken steps to correct them.

- Passive voice makes your writing dull and boggy.

- Passive voice is verbose. Active is crisp.

## Make it easy – I and we

Here's one last trick to see if your sentence is passive. Try to quickly re-write it using either *I* or *we, without changing the order of the words*. If you can't do that, it's probably passive.

~~~~~ **Examples** ~~~~~

**Passive**: The attendees were welcomed by Darth Vader and the speaker was introduced by him. You can't easily turn that into an I-or-we sentence! The attendees were welcomed by I?

119

The speaker was introduced by we??

**Active**: Junior partners bill more than 185 hours per week.

That sentence can easily be written with *I* or *we*: We bill more than 185 hours per week. I bill more than 185 hours per week. (Yes, these sentences are either falsehoods or chicanery, but the point is, they're active.)

~~~~~ ~~~~~ ~~~~~

In the other examples above of active voice, you can easily re-write any of the sentences with an *I* or *we* without changing the order:

- I hoovered up the Pinot Grigio. We hoovered up the Pinot Grigio.

For an enlightening article on passive voice (with generous slashings of vampires and violence) please visit the Resources section of wyws.ca.

A lame rhyme to help you remember

*Checking for passive is e-z*

*Try it out with 'I' or 'we'*

# Open with a bang

It's not easy to open well. Many writers lose their readers by the third or fourth sentence of their message. By the time the writer gets to the third or fourth paragraph – which is when the writer actually gets to the point – they are speaking to dead air.

Let's say you've been asked to find a firm that offers courses in email writing. Below, an example opening paragraph that you find during your online search. After you read it, ask yourself:

- Am I drawn in? Do I feel the writer is speaking to me?

- Am I eager to learn more?

- Do I think the courses will be engaging?

## ~~~~~ Example ~~~~~

**Business Email 101**

Email communication can make or break team unity and project success. Internally, poor email communication can stall or derail many initiatives. Externally, poor email practices can result in customer lack of confidence or trust in the company – a bad impression from a single individual can affect the reputation of the whole enterprise. Our business email course uses time-tested methods to avoid the common mistakes and instill confidence in recipients that the sender (and therefore the company) is receptive and trustworthy.

---

Well? What did you think? Were you drawn in? Now, ask yourself the same questions about the following alternative approach.

---

## Business Email 101

Are you here because:

- Poor email practices are hurting work efficiency in your business?

- Poor email practices are alienating customers?

- A few changes in how your people use email could make a world of difference?

**Our proven, time-tested email course** distills the art of email writing to six easy-to-understand guidelines. In a short time, you'll see a real difference in every course attendee.

You'll have clearer, crisper internal communication, better service, and a better connection to your clients.

~~~~~ ~~~~~ ~~~~~

## Avoid the obvious

The first opening focused blandly on the blandly obvious, on *what readers already know.* Anyone coming to that website is **already thinking of getting email writing help**, that's how they got there! They don't need a lecture on email problems! Starting with the already-known means beginning with the snooze button.

~~~~~ **Example** ~~~~~

Below, two different versions of the opening of a white paper. See what you think.

### Baby Boomers Approaching Retirement

Pentar Consulting has been studying the new retirement challenge by talking to customers, interviewing baby boomers and analyzing survey results. The key takeaway is that a new reality has evolved, where boomers are deviating from conventional retirement paths.

Many no longer plan to retire at or before the age of 65. Many cannot imagine a fulfilling life that does not include paid work. Others, if they want to maintain the lifestyle they have created, cannot afford to retire.

## Boomers versus Retirement

Boomers are a startling 40% of today's workforce. And they don't like getting old. In the same way they used fitness, hair dye, and stolen youth culture to hold onto their prime years, they are now unwilling to go gently into that good night of retirement. Their demographic clout means that this choice will reverberate through HR staffing strategy – but how?

~~~~~ ~~~~~ ~~~~~

Now, put yourself in the place of a senior HR executive. In the first, you're being told that not all boomers are choosing to retire at age 65. Even if there are any people in the business world that don't know this, *none* are senior human resources executives – and they are the crowd at whom such a paper is aimed.

The second opener still refers to the realities of boomers in the workforce. However, it uses a stat the readers might not know (40%) offers specifics rather than generalizations (fitness, hair dye etc.) and some insight to boot. Rather than starting with tired generalizations, it provides a new take and introduces the central theme of the paper (this choice will reverberate through HR staffing strategy).

## Hyphenation

Ages ago, some putz started the rumor that hyphenation was a regulated affair. Subject to known written laws. With every allowable instance recorded ... somewhere.

Not so!

Hyphenated words are one of the rare areas where even the grammar-nazis can't lay a glove on you. The whole thing is just a bit too fuzzzzy. This is totally in your favor. Because hyphens are crazy useful in business writing.

Business writing often pushes you into stringing together several nouns and adjectives. You end up with abominations such as:

- Security enhanced investor prospectus guidelines

- Boutique digital media producer

- Corrosion resistant industrial challenges.

Yikes!

Noun-adjective strings, as above, remind me of a joke in my first joke book:

*Worried woman on bus: I need to get off at Presley Avenue. Do you know where that is?*

*Sally: Sure. Just watch me, and get off the stop before I do.*

In a noun-adjective-string, your reader experiences the same dilemma that *Worried woman on bus* does. Every word EXCEPT the last one serves as a *descriptor*. But the role of each new word is unknown until the final noun is reached. And the final noun is not flagged in any special way.

Your reader's brain has to hold each successive word in temp-think until it can work out the word's role. Is it serving as a noun? An adjective? Something else? Believe me, this is **not** how a reader's mind likes to operate.

Notice how much easier it gets when you call in

hyphen help. Now you can write *Corrosion-resistant industrial challenges typically* …

Bien sûr, some colleague might ask: Is *corrosion-resistant* really a word? Is it in the dictionary?"

You have a few possible answers. The first one, 'Yes,' is best. Others are:

*Who knows?*

*Are you confusing me with someone who cares?*

*Did you get it, or not?*

## ~~~~~ Example ~~~~~

I came across this one on a crowdfunding site:

*A group of networkers meet on Mondays to recite 15 second pitches.*

When I first saw that I thought the networkers were reciting 15 *second* pitches, as opposed to, say, 15 *first* pitches, or 15 *fourth* pitches. Say what?

But see how much clearer it is with a hyphen: A group of networkers meet on Mondays to recite 15-second pitches.

~~~~~ ~~~~~ ~~~~~

Each of the examples I mentioned above is clearer with a hyphen or two:

- Security-enhanced investor-prospectus guidelines

- Boutique digital-media producer

- Corrosion-resistant industrial challenges

## Do you really need that word?

One more suggestion: try to cut words out of the string *before* resorting to hyphen use.

### ~~~~~ Examples ~~~~~

If you're writing about *animal rights protection regulations*, delete the word *protection* and write about *animal rights regulations*. You don't need *protection*; your audience will assume that your goal is to protect the wee critters.

---

In the text above, (*We manufacture custom-engineered solutions to solve corrosion-resistant industrial challenges ...*) delete the word 'industrial' in almost every instance in your document after the first one, because it will be clear from context. You'll end up with (*We manufacture custom-engineered solutions to solve corrosion-resistant challenges ...*)

~~~~~ ~~~~~ ~~~~~

# Avoid starting with a lame comma-separated phrase

I'm convinced it's a hangover from Miss Ledd – that habit of putting the unimportant part of a sentence at the start, set off by commas. It makes weak writers feel like sophisticated ones. In the examples below the result is to send the important part to the arse-end, considerably diluting impact:

~~~~~ Examples ~~~~~

- With the online world becoming more encompassing, Andrew uses his talents to create a gripping web presence for clients.

- Since its founding in 1998 as one of the first control systems integrators in North America, Evactor has become a leading independent provider of process automation solutions.

129

- Business strategist and team builder, Jackson Black offers 15+ years of success in driving market-share capture and strong bottom-line growth.

Put the important part front and center:

- Andrew's strength is in creating a gripping web presence for his clients.

- Evactor is a leading provider of process automation. Since its founding in 1998 as ...

- Jackson Black has been driving market share and bottom-line growth for 15+ years.

What *should* you start with? Try to begin your sentences with subjects and verbs. If it's a longer sentence, make your point early on.

~~~~~ ~~~~~ ~~~~~

# Keep a weather eye out for *ing* and *tion*

Many languages have only one verb-form of the present, but English has three (I write; I am writing; I do write). Stick to the first one (I write) when you can, it will make your voice more direct. *We focus* trumps *We are focusing*.

If you are wondering, by the by, about that third type of present (I do write)? It's used mainly in the negative. I do not sing; I do not dance; I do not act.

Similarly, *tions* have a tendency to muck up your message. *He observed* beats *He made an observation*. When you edit, keep an eye out for *ings* and *tions* and try to weed them out. (I first wrote this sentence as *When you're editing, look for ings and tions and try to weed them out*. Then I revised it…)

## That versus which

Whenever you're unsure whether to choose *that* and *which*, choose *that*. Your chances of being correct are much higher.

Try your hand at the following:

- Baboons [that or which?] don't have red behinds are ostracized by others.

- Salads [that or which?] don't include coriander are second-rate.

- Earth is the only body in the solar system [that or which?] offers ca

*That* is the correct choice in all three.

If you're mad-curious as to those rare times when *which* is appropriate? It's when it introduces a frill, something that the sentence can do without. In the examples below, when you delete the comma-defined part started by *which,* the gist of the meaning remains. *Whiches* are frills.

## ~~~~~ Examples ~~~~~

The salad, *which didn't include coriander*, was second-rate.

The youngest baboon, *which had a turquoise behind*, was ostracized.

~~~~~ ~~~~~ ~~~~~

# All-time easy guide to their, there, they're

Q: What do you say when comforting a grammar-nazi?

A: There, their, they're

Here's your all-time-easy guide to these. And yes, you can find it in the Resources section of wyws.ca any time you need a reminder.

*There* has *here* in it. If you can't substitute the word *here*, don't use *there*. (There's a light, over at the Frankenstein place. There are our friends.)

*Their* has *heir* in it. So ... it refers to owning, to possession ("Teach your children well, *their* father's hell did slowly go by.") My father, your father, their father.

*They're* has an apostrophe, which means it can expand into two words: they are. Only use *they're* when you could also use *they are* (They're not home = They are not home).

~~~~~ **Example** ~~~~~

There is their cottage, *they're* not home.

Notice you could easily say "Here is their cottage, they are not home."

~~~~~ ~~~~~ ~~~~~

# Capitalization

You know you need to capitalize proper names and countries and such. But whenever you're in doubt, do **not** capitalize. Over-capitalization is the mark of an unsophisticated writer.

~~~~~ **Examples** ~~~~~

Incorrect: Did the trainee work in their Marketing Department?

Correct: Did the trainee work in their marketing department?

Incorrect: We are requiring City Taxpayers to pay for unused services.

Correct: We are requiring city taxpayers to pay for unused services.

~~~~~ ~~~~~ ~~~~

*ALL-CAPS*

Capital letters are formal, somewhat forbidding. That's fine in small doses, but you don't want to overdo it. Avoid all-caps ... ALL-CAPS OFTEN TRANSLATE AS SHOUTING. Plus, they're *ineffective*:

- Our eyes *see* lowercase letters far more often than UPPERCASE. We read lowercase letters more easily because we get far more practice with them.

- Lowercase letters give your eye clues by offering a variation in height and placement. Letters such as *a* and *c* use only the mid-space. Others, like *f* and *h* use the mid and the top; *g* and *p* use the mid and bottom. These cues help us read lowercase letters more readily.

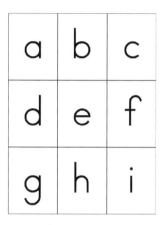

- ALL-CAPS mode is overused by people who want you to pay attention to something you don't care about. *IMPORTANT* stamped on a letter/envelope is my favorite example. When you see it, do you believe it's important? It's smarter to use a touch of **bold** or *italics*. (I avoid using the word *important* in writing.)

## Sentence-case your headers!

Sentence-case headers capitalize only the first word in the header, title-case headers capitalize each word (although not the small ones, typically). For headers, I strongly recommend sentence-case, not title-case. It's more reader-inviting.

~~~~~ **Examples** ~~~~~

Sentence-case: Better quality pays off

Title-case: Capital Letters Seem Forbidding And Old-School

~~~~~ ~~~~~ ~~~~~

*More about capitalization*

A few years ago a businessman wrote a letter to a city's board of education, resigning his post as a director. It had more capital letters strewn about it than a Sesame Street episode. A local blogger got hold of the letter and did a hilarious footnoted analysis. My favorite line was "The shift key is Not a Toy." I still laugh every time I read it.

In addition to being incorrect, over-use of capital letters makes you look inept. Don't go there.

*Scare quotes!*

For reasons I've never understood, some writers think it is 'sophisticated' to use "quotation marks" around 'words' in order to 'emphasize' them. Yes, I'm being 'smartass' right now.

They're called *scare quotes*. When you use scare quotes:

- You look foolish

- You imply that you don't mean what you say. Not a good idea!

### Recommendations

You'll notice that I often use italics instead of single- or double-quotes. Italics look cleaner and less cluttered and they don't trip up the eyes of your reader. I recommend you:

- Use double quotation marks only for actual quotes.

- Use as few single-quotes and double-quotes as possible. They clutter up your writing – particularly doubles.

- Use italics and/or bold when you want to emphasize a word.

Quotes tend to disrupt your reader's attention; do not put quotes around known idioms. **Bad**: Making the machines run optimally is seen as a "black art." **Good**: Making the machines run optimally is seen as a black art.

~~~~~ **Example** ~~~~~

I thought my turn signal wasn't working,

So I asked for help from a friend.

*Go stand behind the car*, I said.

*Let's bring this issue to an end.*


*When I turn the signal on,* said I

*If it's working, let me know.*

I hit the lever. I waited. And heard:

*Yes! No! Yes! No! Yes! No!*

~~~~~ ~~~~~ ~~~~~


*He or she and him or her and all that jazz*
The eagle-eyed among you will have noticed that
I avoid using "he or she" and "his or her" in my
writing. Instead I use the third-person plural:
"they" and "their." Any grammar-stickler worth
their salt can tell you that this is not technically
correct English. Both *they* and *their* should refer to
a plural noun, not a singular one.

Here's the thing: "he or she" and "his or her" are clumsy and awkward. They stop the reader's eye. And I live in horror of stopping my reader's eye; I want my reader to keep reading. And my guess is that my use of *they* and *their* did not stop your eye. My experience is that few if any people notice.

My prediction is that the third-person plural will become the accepted way of dealing with the gender challenge, the clunkiness of sentences such as: *His or her first employee evaluation must be delivered by his or her supervisor within six months of hire date.* Read more about this at www.wyws.ca/resources.

### Apostrophes

If you're not sure if an apostrophe is required and you don't have time for an expert opinion? Leave it out. When in doubt, leave 'em out. Chances of being correct go waaay up. Plus, accidentally-missed apostrophes are often unnoticed, whereas ones that are added but shouldn't be stick out like sore thumbs. [They're called "grocer's apostrophes" because of signs like "Banana's $.90/lb."] Trust me on this one.

### This is very important. Not!

I know I told you earlier that I believe in offering

general principles rather than micro-managing how you write. I'm going to make a tiny exception here and tell you that I'm not fond of the word *very* or the word *important*.

The former is over-used, and it often accomplishes the reverse of what it intends. When you use *very*, you bring in relativity. *He is a happy man* can pack more punch than *He is a very happy man*, because the first is an absolute. And as for *important*, I find that any package or email or communication labeled *important* ... is not. At least not to me. It's only important to the sender.

## Boldface, italics

You learned to write with a pencil and paper, so you didn't have the choice of **boldface** or *italics*. Probably you never developed the habit, you don't turn to them as naturally as you do to all-caps.

**Boldface** and *italics* are excellent ways to emphasize. Resolve to use them more. Above all, use **boldface**:

- In emails, for deadlines and/or action items.

- In website copy, to draw your reader's flighty eye to the things you need them to see.

## Justifying text

Full-justified text works for published hard-copy books, partly because they use sophisticated software. It doesn't work in Microsoft Word – you end up with large ugly gaps between words. Worse yet, full-justified text subtly encourages you to create those solid blocks of boxy text that Miss Ledd loved so well.

Don't go there. Do not full-justify your text. Ragged-right margin (aka left-justified) appeals considerably more to a reader's eye. Or as my graphic artist Jessica says: *Full justified makes it look like homework.*

## Packing a punch with simple text

It's an urban legend that New Yorker Hugh Gallagher wrote the following as a college entrance essay. But he did write it in high school, and he did win a national writing contest with it.

As you read this essay, note the:

- Use of simple words that pack a punch: Using only a hoe and a large glass of water, I once single-handedly defended a small village.

- Many short sentences: I don't perspire. I am a private citizen, yet I receive fan mail. Children trust me.

- Simple style.

- Use of startling juxtaposition: I am an expert in stucco, a veteran in love, and an outlaw in Peru.

- Use of the concrete rather than the intangible: I can hurl tennis rackets at small moving objects with deadly accuracy.

- Power of the final, one-sentence paragraph.

## ~~~~~ Example ~~~~~

I am a dynamic figure, often seen scaling walls and crushing ice. I have been known to remodel train stations on my lunch breaks, making them more efficient in the area of heat retention. I translate ethnic slurs for Cuban refugees, I write award-winning operas, I manage time efficiently.

Occasionally, I tread water for three days in a row. I woo women with my sensuous and godlike trombone playing, I can pilot bicycles up severe inclines with unflagging speed, and I cook Thirty-Minute Brownies in twenty minutes. I am an expert in stucco, a veteran in love, and an outlaw in Peru.

Using only a hoe and a large glass of water, I once single-handedly defended a small village in the Amazon Basin from a horde of ferocious army ants. I play bluegrass cello, I was scouted by the Mets, I am the subject of numerous documentaries. When I'm bored, I build large suspension bridges in my yard. I enjoy urban hang gliding. On Wednesdays, after school, I repair electrical appliances free of charge.

I am an abstract artist, a concrete analyst, and a ruthless bookie. Critics worldwide swoon over my original line of corduroy evening wear. I don't perspire. I am a private citizen, yet I receive fan mail. I have been caller number nine and have won the weekend passes. Last summer I toured New Jersey with a traveling centrifugal-force demonstration. I bat 400.

My deft floral arrangements have earned me

fame in international botany circles. Children trust me. I can hurl tennis rackets at small moving objects with deadly accuracy. I once read Paradise Lost, Moby Dick, and David Copperfield in one day and still had time to refurbish an entire dining room that evening. I know the exact location of every food item in the supermarket. I have performed several covert operations with the CIA.

I sleep once a week; when I do sleep, I sleep in a chair. While on vacation in Canada, I successfully negotiated with a group of terrorists who had seized a small bakery. I balance, I weave, I dodge, I frolic, and my bills are all paid.

On weekends, to let off steam, I participate in full-contact origami. Years ago I discovered the meaning of life but forgot to write it down. I have made extraordinary four course meals using only a mouli and a toaster oven. I breed prize-winning clams. I have won bullfights in San Juan, cliff-diving competitions in Sri Lanka, and spelling bees at the Kremlin.

I have played Hamlet, I have performed open-heart surgery, and I have spoken with Elvis.

But I have not yet gone to college.

~~~~~ ~~~~~ ~~~~~

## The *visual* and the *heard*

*The Visual And The Heard ... doesn't that sound like an Aesop's fable? ... e.g. One day a Visual was walking towards a herd of ...*

Most of us think of reading as a mental activity. We don't get the visual and aural/audio aspects. But the visual is more important than you think! And the aural, surprisingly, plays a role as well.

Give your reader shorter paragraphs, varying in size (aka lots of white space), with occasional use of bullet points, and you'll be presenting an inviting visual. They'll be more likely to start; they'll be more likely to continue.

Aural is tougher. Don't worry about it unless you're writing something that really matters to your work. But studies have shown that people 'hear' the aural quality of writing, the spoken quality, even when it's not read aloud. It comes out in cadence.

So when it's a piece that matters, read the first draft aloud when you've completed it. You'll get clues from that as to how to improve it.

# Emails!

Emails were the first writing form of the digital world. No wonder so many get them wrong – most are applying Robert's Rules of Order to a light-saber skirmish.

What are the common mistakes? And what are the remedies? Following, a brief review. Also, you can download my one-pager on email-writing in the Resources section of wyws.ca.

### Length and paragraphing

Two things to know:

1. People *scan* your emails at light-speed. The growth of texting and tweeting has doubled-down on this reality.

2. Your reader almost always quits after the first point in your email. Don't ask me why. But they do. Every time!

Therefore:

- Your emails (95% of the time) should be **at most** a few sentences long. And have **one** (1) point. Need to write more than that? Put the rest in an attachment doc, with the critical message in the email document. Or write a second email. Or even a series of emails.

- You want to discuss more than one point? Create another email.

My colleague Sid once said to me, "You know those lonnng emails from J— - in Chicago? When I get one, I read the first sentence, take a quick scan through to see if my name is mentioned anywhere, check out the closing, and get on with my day."

### Short paragraphs – for emails

**Q**: How long should a paragraph be **in an email**?

**A**: One to two sentences. Three at a stretch. Email paragraphs are *even shorter* than regular paragraphs.

Be comfortable sending an email that consists of three one-sentence paragraphs. I do it all the time. **With email, the regular rules don't apply**. The one rule that does apply is: *Move it forward*. Whatever goal you're trying to accomplish, move it one step closer with your email.

~~~~~ Examples ~~~~~

Here's a good email. The writer has used all kinds of things that I recommend, e.g. putting things like timing info in point-form at the top, using headers like *Purpose,* and using *italics* to make critical things jump out.

---

Hi everyone,

Thanks for agreeing to join the session.

**Timing**: Start at 5:30, end about 7:30

**Location**: Angela and Barb's office, 179 Shuter, Suite 400

**Purpose**: Help Angela and Barb define their **Changing Patterns** business offering. Now that they've launched their book, they've decided to focus on **Changing Patterns** as their main business venture.

Angela and Barb have the classic problem of knowing exactly what they do, but finding it difficult to *articulate* the process, benefits and results.

Below, links to all the relevant web sites I'm aware of.

This should be fun! I've heard rumors that

gourmet fare will be supplied.

See you all Wednesday.

Regards,

Salah

~~~~~ ~~~~~ ~~~~~

## *Subject line! Subject line! Subject line!*
Nothing matters more than the subject line.

Yet most of us blow by it. **Not** a good idea! It's fine once you've got a thread established, but if you're starting a fresh email, or changing the thread, **nothing matters more**.

Your audience's first question is: *What's this about?* Answer that question in the subject line if you can.

Also, recall how headers or sub-headers are more powerful if they are **not** blandly descriptive? That they work better if they are calls to action or attempts to draw in the reader?

Subject lines are the same. Think about your subject line, for, say, 5-30 seconds, every time. You'll get faster and better at it, I promise.

And as for not having a subject line? *Please*

people. Let's not even go there.

| Weak subject | Strong subject |
|---|---|
| New phones | What you need to do before Feb. 28 phone installation |
| Next steps | Next steps: Compliance meetings in April – dates for your calendar |
| Registration fee | Response to your inquiry re: Con Max registration fee |

## *Context in emails – do it quickly at the outset*

Your reader is getting emails and other communications from every direction. Misunderstandings abound. If your email is not part of a continued conversation, provide context **at the outset** to help your reader quickly understand what you are writing about.

## *Clear calls to action*

Let your readers know what action is required, early on. **Boldface** any call to action or point that you want to be sure your reader gets. Note that they will love you for this when they go back to your email 2 minutes before the related meeting.

~~~~~ **Examples** ~~~~~

*Email to a Board of Directors*

The attached report updates the status of construction, which is *on* schedule but running *over* budget. We will discuss **report highlights** at next week's meeting on **April 18**.

*Email to a colleague*

Horace, here are last month's sales figures. Please **review and approve by Feb 3** so I can send them out to the group.

~~~~~ ~~~~~ ~~~~~

*If your email has a life expectancy of over a week...*

If your email might be passed on to many others, or live into the future, beef it up a bit context-wise. Make sure any dates include years; add a sentence or para at the opening to clarify context. Avoid acronyms.

# Writing about numbers

It's hard to write about numbers. Readers' eyes glaze. Memory and attention dial-down fast.

Here are a couple of tricks:

1. Use percentages, not raw figures. I'm astonished how often reporters quote raw figures rather than percentages (*Global expenditures on xxx in 2015 were $189,306 versus $139,254 in 2014*). Isn't it far more meaningful to read that *Expenditures in 2015 were $192,300, a 36% increase from 2014*?

2. Try to make the numbers real. Put them in context, e.g. "This $15,000,000 expenditure represents ¼ of our capital budget for the year."

Here's my all-time-fave example of portraying numbers well. It's an email that wound its way around the globe a few times in 2013.

## ~~~~~ Example ~~~~~

### US national debt:

- U.S. Tax revenue: $2,170,000,000,000

- Fed budget: $3,820,000,000,000

- New debt: $ 1,650,000,000,000

- National debt: $14,271,000,000,000

- Recent budget cuts: $ 38,500,000,000

**Let's now remove 8 zeros and pretend it's a household budget:**

- Annual family income: $21,700

- Money the family spent: $38,200

- New debt on the credit card: $16,500

- Outstanding balance on the credit card: meaning$142,710

- Total budget cuts: $385

~~~~~ ~~~~~ ~~~~~

## "Why can't we just say that?"

Some of you might be thinking that the type of writing I advocate in this book is only appropriate for internal communication, for informal business situations.

Maybe.

But I'd argue that the world is moving, every day, to a more relaxed style of business writing. Even in that last bastion of complex turgid prose: legal documents.

I had a convo about this recently with my tax

accountant, one of the smartest people I know. She's often involved in the task of producing commercial leases. She tells me that someone in the room will often ask the lawyer: "This piece here – what's the translation?"

Once the lawyer decodes what the piece of text means, in plain English, the questioner will often say: "Why can't we just say that?"

And they do.

~~~~~ **One last example** ~~~~~

Steve Jobs' resignation letter was perfectly aligned with the sleek design of his devices. It also shows his awareness of the human element that Stephen Fry speaks of as being Jobs' trademark. Notice the powerful closing comment about the 'best friends of his life.' You could run a whole writing workshop on the things Steve did right in this letter.

Note also the increased power that results from the letter being so simple, so spare, so whitespace-aware. Don't think that Jobs had nothing more to say! He did. He just edited out anything that wasn't critical to the message.

Result? You read it. You get it. You remember it. Nice job, Mr. Jobs.

## To the Apple Board of Directors and the Apple Community:

I have always said if there ever came a day when I could no longer meet my duties and expectations as Apple's CEO, I would be the first to let you know. Unfortunately, that day has come.

I hereby resign as CEO of Apple. I would like to serve, if the Board sees fit, as Chairman of the Board, director and Apple employee.

As far as my successor goes, I strongly recommend that we execute our succession plan and name Tim Cook as CEO of Apple.

I believe Apple's brightest and most innovative days are ahead of it. And I look forward to watching and contributing to its success in a new role.

I have made some of the best friends of my life at Apple, and I thank you all for the many years of being able to work alongside you.

Steve

~~~~~ ~~~~~ ~~~~~

# Conclusion

Go easy on yourself, you don't have to do it all at once.

BARF-ing … learning to self-edit ruthlessly and often … getting comfortable with simpler sentences … give yourself some time to adopt these new practices. Focus on just one in any given week.

The good news? The practices you've been reading about will help you to write more effectively *and* more easily. By following the *Why Your Writing Sucks* approach to writing, you will not only raise your value in the workplace, you will make your work life a little easier.

Go forth and conquer.

# Acknowledgements

Encouragement. Support. Proofing. Champagne. Developmental edit. Ideas. Reviewing. Faith. Patience. Laughter. Did I say support already?

Bob McKnight, Charlene Norman, Cheryl Finch, Deb O'Neill, Don Ross, Emer Killean, Graham Zimmerman, Hilary Holden, Jessica Heald, Margo Zimmerman, Marlene Nyilassy, Phil Anderson, Sid Ouagague, Sonia Marques, Steve Garrett, Suzanne Tyson, Wesley Stevens. And Mum and Dad of course.

Thank you thank you thank you. Thank you.

# About the author

Marcia Ross combines a love of the written word with a fascination for anything business. She consults, coaches and presents on every aspect of business communication. She also serves as V.P. Content for Imaginis Business Development, and is a past board member of the Toronto chapter of IABC (International Association of Business Communicators).

Marcia holds an honours B.A. in History from Queen's University and an MBA from the Richard Ivey School of Business. She has three grown children. She lives in Toronto beside her sports club, so she won't have to stock shampoo and towels at home.

Learn more about Marcia and *Why Your Writing Sucks* at www.wyws.ca

Made in the USA
Middletown, DE
12 July 2022

69107902R00093